CHAMPIONS OF FREEDOM

The Ludwig von Mises Lecture Series

CHAMPIONS OF FREEDOM
Volume 30

Free Markets or Bureaucracy?
Economic Problem-Solving
in the 21st Century

Richard M. Ebeling
Editor

Hillsdale College Press
Hillsdale, Michigan 49242

Hillsdale College Press

CHAMPIONS OF FREEDOM
The Ludwig von Mises Lecture Series—Volume 30
Free Markets or Bureaucracy?
Economic Problem-Solving in the 21st Century

©2003 Hillsdale College Press, Hillsdale, Michigan 49242

First printing 2003

Printed in the United States of America

Front cover: © Sanford/Agliolo/CORBIS

Library of Congress Control Number 2002116819
ISBN 0-916308-53-7

Contents

Contributors

SALLIE BALIUNAS, an astrophysicist at the Harvard-Smithsonian Center for Astrophysics and Deputy Director of Mount Wilson Observatory, received her M.A. and Ph.D. degrees in astrophysics from Harvard University. Dr. Baliunas is co-host of the Website <www.TechCentralStation.com> and leads its Enviro-Sci corner. She serves as Senior Scientist at the George C. Marshall Institute in Washington, D.C. Past contributing editor to the *World Climate Report*, she is receiving editor for *New Astronomy*. Her awards include the Newton-Lacy-Pierce Prize of the American Astronomical Society, the Petr Beckmann Award for Scientific Freedom, and the Bok Prize from Harvard University. The author of over 200 scientific research articles, *Discover* magazine profiled her as one of America's outstanding women scientists in 1991. She also served as technical consultant for a science-fiction television series, *Gene Roddenberry's "Earth: Final Conflict."* Dr. Baliunas's research interests include solar variability and other factors in climate change, magnetohydrodynamics of the sun and sunlike stars, expoplanets, and the use of laser electrooptics for the correction of turbulence due to the earth's atmosphere in astronomical images.

RICHARD M. EBELING is the Ludwig von Mises Professor of Economics at Hillsdale College. In addition, he serves as vice president of The Future of Freedom Foundation and writes for its monthly magazine, *Freedom Daily*. He has edited several books, including *The Dangers of Socialized Medicine* (Future of Freedom Foundation, 1994), *The Tyranny of Gun Control* (Future of Freedom Foundation, 1997), and a number of volumes in the Hillsdale College Press series Champions of Freedom. A collection of his essays are being published under the title *Austrian Economics and the Political Economy of Freedom* (Edward Elgar, 2003). He has lectured extensively on privatization and monetary reform throughout the United States, Latin America, and the former Soviet Union, where he has consulted with the Lithuanian government, the city of Moscow, and the Russian parliament. Currently he is writing a biography of Ludwig von Mises and editing a series of volumes that will feature Mises' recently unearthed pre-World War II papers. Two of the planned three volumes have been published: *Selected Writings of Ludwig von Mises,* Vol. 3; *The Political Economy of International Reform and Reconstruction* (2000) and Vol. 2: *Between the Two World Wars: Monetary Disorder, Interventionism, Socialism and the Great Depression* (2002).

EDWARD J. ERLER, professor of Political Science at California State University, San Bernardino, received his Ph.D. from Claremont Graduate School. He is the author of *The American Polity: Essays on the Theory and Practice of Constitutional Government* (Crane Russak, 1991) and numerous articles in political philosophy and constitutional law. Among his most recent works are "From Subjects to Citizens: The Social Contract Origins of American Citizenship"; "Crime, Punishment and Romero: An Analysis of the Case Against California's Three Strikes Law"; and "Californians and Their Constitution: Progressivism, Direct Democracy and the Administrative State." Dr. Erler has also been a member of the California Advisory Commission on Civil Rights since 1988 and served on the California Constitutional Revision Commission in 1996. He recently traveled to Iran.

PETER FERRARA, director of the International Center for Law and Economics, is a graduate of Harvard College and Harvard Law School. He has written numerous books, studies, and articles on Social Security, including The Cato Institute's first book on the subject, *Social Security: The Inherent Contradiction* (Cato Institute, 1980). Mr. Ferrara is the co-author, with Michael Tanner, of *A New Deal for Social Security* (Cato Institute, 1998) and *Common Cents, Common Dreams* (Cato Institute, 1998), both presenting the case for a private option to Social Security. Mr. Ferrara served as a senior staff member in the Reagan White House Office of Policy Development from 1981 to 1983. He was Associate Professor of Law at the George Mason University School of Law from 1987 to 1991, and Associate Deputy Attorney General of the United States from 1991 to 1993.

STEVEN HAYWARD, a senior fellow and director of the Center for Environmental Studies at the Pacific Research Institute for Public Policy in San Francisco and the Weyerhaeuser Fellow of the American Enterprise Institute in Washington, D.C., received his M.A. in government and Ph.D. in American studies from Claremont Graduate School. He is the principal author of *The Index of Leading Environmental Indicators*, released each year on Earth Day, and he served on the Bush–Cheney transition team for the Environmental Protection Agency. During 1997–1998, he was also a visiting fellow at the Heritage Foundation in Washington, D.C., where he studied urban issues. He has testified about urban sprawl before the U.S. Senate, has been interviewed for a PBS-TV documentary about sprawl, and appeared on *The News Hour with Jim Lehrer*. He writes frequently on a wide range of topics for such publications as *National Review*, the *Weekly Standard*, the *New York Times*, and *The Wall Street Journal*. He is the author or co-author of six books, including *The Age of Reagan: The Fall of the Old Liberal Order, 1964–1980* (Prima, 2001), the first of two volumes about Ronald Reagan's legacy. Dr. Hayward is at work on a book to be titled *The Unheavenly Suburb: The Controversy Over Urban Sprawl.*

MARK R. LEVIN received his B.A. from Temple University, where he graduated Phi Beta Kappa and magna cum laude, and his J.D. from Temple University School of Law, and is now president of Landmark Legal Foundation. He has worked as an attorney in the private sector and as a top advisor and administrator to several members of President Ronald Reagan's Cabinet. He served as chief of staff to the Attorney General of the United States, deputy assistant secretary for elementary and secondary education at the U.S. Department of Education, and deputy solicitor of the U.S. Department of the Interior. He was also elected to the Cheltenham Township (Pennsylvania) School Board. The American Conservative Union (ACU) Foundation named Mr. Levin the recipient of the 2001 Ronald Reagan Award, which is the highest honor bestowed by the ACU Foundation, one of the oldest and most highly regarded organizations in the conservative movement.

MICHAEL LYNCH, a contributing editor for *Reason* magazine, received his B.A. in political science from the University of Washington and an M.A. in economics from San Francisco State University. He also writes for such newspapers and magazines as *The Wall Street Journal, San Francisco Chronicle,* the *Weekly Standard, Investor's Business Daily,* and *Chief Executive.* He has served as the Washington editor of *Reason,* as a senior public policy fellow at the Pacific Research Institute, and as a research associate at the Washington Institute for Policy Studies in Seattle, Washington. He makes frequent radio and television appearances, and has guest lectured at the University of California at Berkeley, San Francisco State University, and the City College of San Francisco. Mr. Lynch has been a Publius Fellow at the Claremont Institute for the Study of Statesmanship and Political Philosophy, and has received two Felix Morley Memorial Prizes in journalism from the Institute for Humane Studies, in 1993 and 1994, and the 1994 John B. Wood award from London's Institute for Economic Affairs for his writing on environmentalism.

LAWRENCE M. STRATTON, a graduate of the Georgetown University Law Center, the University of Pennsylvania's Wharton School of Finance, and Princeton Theological Seminary, is a fellow at the Institute for Political Economy. Mr. Stratton is the co-author, with Paul Craig Roberts, of *The New Color Line: How Quotas and Privilege Destroy Democracy* (Regnery, 1997) and *The Tyranny of Good Intentions: How Prosecutors and Bureaucrats are Trampling the Constitution in the Name of Justice* (Prima, 2000). A member of the bar in the District of Columbia and Virginia, he has taught constitutional law at Georgetown University Law Center and served as a judicial clerk to Federal District Judge Claude M. Hilton of the U.S. District Court for the Eastern District of Virginia. Currently, he is a Ph.D. candidate in ethics at Princeton Theological Seminary. He has testified before the Judiciary Committees of the U.S. House of Representatives and the California State Assembly. Mr. Stratton has been a speaker at numerous institutions, including Columbia Law School, the University of Pennsylvania, Syracuse University, and Georgetown University.

MALCOLM WALLOP is chairman of Frontiers of Freedom Institute, the Chung Ju-Yung Fellow for Policy Studies at the Heritage Foundation, and a former Republican Senator from Wyoming. After receiving his B.A. from Yale University, he served in the U.S. Army as a First Lieutenant and in the Wyoming Legislature. He was subsequently elected to the United States Senate in 1976, where he served for eighteen years, sitting on numerous committees, including the Finance Committee, Small Business Committee, the Armed Services Committee, and the Select Committee on Intelligence. As the ranking Republican member of the Energy and Natural Resources Committee from 1990 to 1994, Senator Wallop was an outspoken advocate of the multiple economic uses of federal lands. His numerous legislative achievements include the adoption of the "Wallop Amendment" to the 1980 Clean Water Act, barring federal usurpation of state control of water. A highly regarded arms control expert, he has lectured widely on defense issues in America, England, Belgium, and France, and is the co-author, with Angelo Codevilla, of *The Arms Control Delusion* (Institute for Contemporary Studies, 1987). His articles have appeared in numerous publications, including the *Strategic Review, National Review,* the *Notre Dame Law School Journal, National Interest, The Wall Street Journal,* the *New York Times,* and *USA Today.* He has been a guest on *Nightline, The Today Show,* and *CBS Morning News.* His many awards include the American Conservative Union's John Ashbrook Award and Ronald Reagan Award, the National Federation of Independent Business's Guardian of Small Business Award, and an award from the American League of Anglers and Boaters. An active businessman, Senator Wallop sits on the boards of Hubbell, Inc. and El Paso Energy Partners, and is the President of Eaglestone Plastics, Inc.

Foreword

This is the 30th volume in the Hillsdale College Press series Champions of Freedom. Compiled from the Ludwig von Mises Lecture series, which has been held for three decades at the College, Champions of Freedom was begun under the presidency of George Roche III. George began his career at the Foundation for Economic Education where he became an admirer and a colleague of Ludwig von Mises.

Hillsdale College was built under the influence of the American Revolution. In that revolution there was much talk of property rights. These are rights, said Madison, to the material things that we have made and earned. These are also rights to every natural property that belongs to the human being. This means his ability to think and to speak. It means his capacity to worship the Almighty, and his individual responsibility to that highest Being. Property rights are a kind of summation of all of our rights.

In modern times, many great economists have worked to recover the full force of this powerful view, which has been the chief foundation of liberty in the modern world. Among these economists, none is more important than the great Ludwig von Mises.

Hillsdale College has a special connection to Mises. He gave us his personal library, and in making this splendid gift he said these fine words: "Hillsdale, more than any other educational institution, most strongly represents the free market ideas to which I have given my life."

LARRY P. ARNN
President
Hillsdale College

Introduction

The examples of bureaucratic control over social life seem to be as old as recorded history, and they always have features and characteristics that seem universal in their application, regardless of time and place. In his classic history of the ancient Inca Empire in Peru, the noted French economist and social philosopher Louis Baudin described the structure of its bureaucratic system:

> Every socialist system must rest upon a powerful bureaucratic administration. In the Inca Empire, as soon as a province was conquered, its population would be organized on a hierarchical basis, and the officials would immediately set to work. . . . The responsibilities of all these officials extended over an extremely broad field. They were in general in charge of the preparation of the statistical tables, the requisitioning of the supplies and provisions needed by their group [over whom they ruled] (seeds, staple foods, wool, etc.), the distribution of the production of the products obtained, the solicitation of assistance and relief in case of need, the supervision of the conduct of their inferiors, and the rendering of complete reports and accounts to their superiors. These operations were facilitated by the fact that those under their supervision were obliged to admit them to their homes at any moment, and allow them to inspect everything in their homes, "down to the cooking utensils," and even to eat "with the doors open.". . . [The administrative official] not only oversees the work done and made sure that the workers received adequate

maintenance, but was obliged to denounce delinquents and demand their punishment. . . . The particular responsibility of the
higher officials was to supervise the collection of taxes. . . . The
whole system was kept under the watchful eyes of inspectors who
made general tours of the empire every three years. . . . Finally,
the officials of all ranks were expected to gather vital statistics,
arrange marriages, and punish delinquents.[1]

Baudin explained that the Inca bureaucracy cast its net over all
those that it ruled and soon transformed them into docile and obedient subjects through "a slow and gradual absorption of the individual
into the state . . . until it brought about the loss of personality. Man
was made for the state, and not the state for the man." The Incas did
this, Baudin said, by banishing "the two great causes of popular disaffection, *poverty* and *idleness*, and they left only a small place for ambition and greed. But, by the same token, they dried up the two springs
of progress, *initiative* and a *provident concern for the future.*" The regi-
mentation was so comprehensive over every facet of life that "[t]he
Indian did not have to do any thinking for himself. The government
thought and acted for him, and if its actions were suspended, social
life would stop short. Under the rule of the Incas the inertia expressed
itself in the stagnation of commerce . . . in the lack of vitality and the
absence of originality in the arts, in dogmatism in science, and in the
rareness of even the simplest of inventions."[2]

This inertia was fostered through the institutions of the welfare
state. "As for the provident concern for the future," Baudin asked,
"how could that have been developed among a people whose public
granaries were crammed with provisions and whose public officials
were authorized to distribute them in case of need? There was never
any need to think beyond the necessities of the moment." In addition, the Inca welfare state undermined the spirit and the motive for
charity and any personal sense of responsibility for family or community members:

But what is even more serious is that the substitution of the
state for the individual in the economic domain destroyed the
spirit of charity. The native Peruvian, expecting the state to do

everything, no longer had to concern himself with his fellow man and had to come to his aid only if required by law. The members of a community were compelled to work on the land for the benefit of those who were incapacitated; but when this task had been performed, they were free from all further obligations. They had to help their neighbors if ordered to do so by their chiefs, but they were obliged to do nothing on their own initiative. That is why, by the time of the Spanish conquest, the most elementary humanitarian feelings were in danger of disappearing entirely.[3]

Life was also reduced to a joyless existence of uniformity, security, and order that was imposed and guaranteed by the Inca bureaucracy:

Was the Indian happy? . . . He labored contentedly for a master whom he held to be divine. He had only to obey, without going to the trouble of thinking. If his horizon was limited, he was unaware of it, since he knew no other; and if he could not raise himself socially, he in no way suffered on that account, for he did not conceive that such a rise was possible. His life followed its peaceful course, its monotony broken by periodic holiday festivals and by such events as marriages, military service, and compulsory labor service, all in strict accordance with regulations. The Indian had his joys and sorrows at fixed dates. Only illness and death persisted in escaping government regulation. . . . It was a negative kind of happiness, with few great adversities and few great joys. The empire produced what D'Argenson called the "menagerie of happy men.". . . The Indian's soul was lulled to sleep by the monotonous rhythm of a too well regulated existence. . . . In the Inca state only the members of the ruling class, and more especially, the chief, could live a full life; outside of him and his family, men were no longer men, but cogs in the economic machine or figures in the official statistics.[4]

In our time, the plague of bureaucracy has been no different. Those who man the bureaucratic agencies supervise and oversee many, if not most, of our economic affairs from the processes of production to the stage at which we actually use the goods that are manufactured. They pry into and then proceed to regulate our private, personal, and family affairs. They take responsibility for our welfare and our happiness, and try to guard us against any of the trials and tribulations of everyday life. They watch over our schooling, care for us when we are ill, find work for us if we are unemployed, and pay us when we are without a job. They are concerned about our mental health and police what we ingest in our bodies. They take an interest in the things we read and the amusements and leisure activities we indulge in.

Even America, that land that is so much freer than many other parts of the world, particularly in its economic affairs, has slowly over the decades been enveloped within the arms of the paternalism of the bureaucratic state. One freedom after another has been incrementally abridged, weakened, and then passed away with the government's bureaucracy now in charge and responsible for what had previously been in the domain of the individual and his personal arena of choice and action. But in this, too, the process has been no different than under the Incas of Peru. Louis Baudin pointed out that, "The poison [of growing bureaucratic paternalism] was not given to the Indians in massive doses that would have provoked a reaction, but was administered drop by drop, until it brought about the loss of personality.... [A]nd whoever has formed the habit of passive obedience ends by being no longer able to act for himself and comes to love the yoke that is laid upon him. Nothing is easier than to obey a master who is perhaps exacting, but who rules over all the details of life, assure one's daily bread, and makes it possible to banish all concern from the mind."[5]

In fact, the human spirit and will are not so easily and permanently broken as the Incas believed they had succeeded in doing in Peru centuries ago. In our own time, we have witnessed that individuals cherished their individuality and retained the desire for freedom even after three generations of communist rule in Russia, under which there had been the attempt, too, to reduce man to a docile component in the collective body.[6]

The 2002 Ludwig von Mises Lecture Series, held at Hillsdale College, was devoted to the theme "Free Markets or Bureaucracy? Economic Problem-Solving in the 21st Century." The speakers participating in the program each focused upon a separate aspect of government regulation and bureaucratic control that has generated inefficiencies, economic waste, misdirected incentives, corrupt practices, and concentrations of power in the hands of the political authority. And the speakers, whose contributions are contained in this volume, all attempted to offer market-oriented alternatives to the clumsy and rough embrace of government around the private sector.

The contrast between private enterprise and bureaucratic management was a topic that Ludwig von Mises, in whose name these lectures are delivered each year, discussed numerous times over his long scholarly life. Mises explained the distinction between these two methods of organizing economic activities in an extremely concise manner in an article that he wrote in 1930:

> Commercial business management reflects the nature of private enterprise, while bureaucratic business management is in line with the nature of officialdom, which administers the affairs of the State. The commercial enterprise has as its compass nothing except the profitability of its business. The entrepreneur of a private firm gives the employees, to whom he transfers various independent tasks, one single instruction: to strive for the maximization of profit. In this directive is contained all that he has to say to them, and the system of accounting is then able to determine easily and readily to what degree the instruction has been fulfilled.
>
> The manager of a public agency or bureau finds himself in a completely different situation, since the success or failure of official activities cannot be evaluated by the same bookkeeping and auditing methods. He can give his subordinates orders about what they are expected to do, but he cannot check to see whether the resources that they spent to achieve this result are in proper relationship to the goal. If he is not omni-

present in all the agencies and bureaus under his supervision, then he is not able to judge whether or not the same result could have been accomplished with a smaller expenditure of labor and material resources. Since an arithmetical assessment in the same form as commercial bookkeeping is impossible for the determination of this relationship between ends and means, the manager of a bureaucratic organization must supply his subordinates with instructions for the carrying out of the duties for which they are responsible.

In these instructions provisions are made, in a schematic way, for the carrying out of the ordinary and routine operation of the public enterprise. But for all extraordinary situations, before expenditures can be made, the superior authority's approval must be obtained. This may be a sluggish and inefficient procedure, but it is the only one possible in these circumstances. After all, if every subordinate agency, department, branch-office were given the right to make those expenditures that were considered necessary, then the administrative costs would rise without limit. We cannot ignore the fact that this system is highly defective and very far from being satisfactory. Consent is frequently given to superfluous expenditures and many needed expenditures are not permitted, precisely because, given the nature of the bureaucratic apparatus, it is unable to adapt to changing circumstances as readily as can the commercial sector.[7]

The choice that any society has is either a system of free market capitalism or government control and regulation. In the free market all of the productive activities of the society are harnessed to satisfy the demands of the consuming public as reflected in their willingness to purchase goods and services at various competitively established prices. Business enterprises pursue the earning of profit by applying the resources, capital equipment, and labor services at their disposal in ways that produce the supplies of those things the entrepreneurs believe the consumers are interested in buying. If they fail in this task they run the risk of suffering losses instead of earning profits. And if losses persist, the ownership and control of the enterprise's assets pass into the hands of others who will try to more effectively serve those consumers. The profit and loss system acts as the steering mechanism and the discipline to make activities of private producers conform to the desires of the consumers in the society—which is ultimately all of us who earn income in our production roles in the market, which enables us to purchase the goods and services that our fellow men are offering to sell to us.

The society, on the other hand, can be organized along bureaucratic lines. If economic activities are completely bureaucratized then the society lives under some form of socialism, under which the government directly owns and/or controls the means of production and determines all that gets produced and the relative shares of the output each member of the society will be given. Or the society can be partially bureaucratized through an extensive network of government controls, regulations, restrictions, and compulsions. The market economy is not abolished, but it is restrained, hampered, and deflected from the production and consumption paths that would be followed if the resources, capital, and labor of the society were strictly applied by private producers to serve the demands of the buying public. Political ideology and special interest politics then influence the patterns and direction of all market activity, and not the voluntary choices of each of us in the process of peaceful and noncoercive exchange.

The Hillsdale College Press publishes these lectures as part of its Champions of Freedom series to widen the debate on markets versus bureaucracy with the hope that in this new century the path of prosperity through freedom will be once again followed, not only in America but around the world.

RICHARD M. EBELING
Ludwig von Mises Professor
of Economics
Hillsdale College

Notes

[1] Louis Baudin, *A Socialist Empire: The Incas of Peru* [1928] (Princeton, NJ: D. Van Nostrand, 1961), pp. 134–36.

[2] Ibid., pp. 199–200.

[3] Ibid., p. 202.

[4] Ibid., pp. 206–8.

[5] Ibid., pp. 199–200.

[6] See Mikhail Heller, *Cogs in the Wheel: The Formation of Soviet Man* (New York: Alfred A. Knopf, 1988).

[7] Ludwig von Mises, "Commercial and Bureaucratic Business Management" [1930] in Richard M. Ebeling, ed., *Selected Writings of Ludwig von Mises*, Vol. 2. *Between the Two World Wars: Monetary Disorder, Interventionism, Socialism, and the Great Depression* (Indianapolis, IN: Liberty Fund, 2002), pp. 163–64.

Richard M. Ebeling

The Market Economy and the Political Process: Self-Government, Bureaucracy, and Interventionism

Self-Government in the Political Arena and in the Marketplace

The twentieth century was most certainly the most inhuman and brutal one hundred years in modern history. Two world wars as well as the Nazi and Communist forms of totalitarianism have been estimated to have caused the death of at least 250 million people. This would be equivalent to the mass murder of almost the entire combined populations of France, Italy, Germany, and the United Kingdom.

Freedom in all its forms was sacrificed on the altar of nationalism, imperialism, racism, and class warfare. Tyrants and dictators claimed that all their actions were in the name of the people and for the interest of the masses. But the common characteristic of both totalitarian and authoritarian regimes in the twentieth century was their rejection of the right of the people to demonstrate their desires and preferences through the democratic voting process. Democracy was condemned as divisive and corrupt. Democracy was declared to be an illusion of freedom, through which powerful social and economic interests manipulated the political system for their own benefit at the expense of the rest of the society.

The rejection of totalitarian and authoritarian regimes around the world has represented a rebirth of the ideal of the democratic

1

order. Hundreds of millions of people have declared their belief in their ability to rule the political affairs of their own countries. The people of the world have proclaimed their dedication to self-government. But it is important to remember that "self-government" can and has meant two different, but complementary, ideals.

Self-government in the political sense means that the members of society shall have the right to participate in and decide through the electoral process who holds office in the government. The people shall choose those who will enact and enforce the laws of the land. The role of political self-government is to assure that those who administer the state are accountable to those they represent. Periodic elections enable the people to judge the continuing fitness and integrity of the elected officials, and to help prevent abuses of power.

Political self-government also serves as a means of changing both the men and the policies that rule the society without recourse to violent revolution or civil war. Democracy introduces civil peace into the political process by eliminating the necessity of taking up arms to remove those in high office. Death and destruction are no longer the price for political change.

But there is a second definition of self-government. This refers to the self-governing individual. The great ideal of the classical liberal thinkers of the eighteenth and nineteenth centuries was that the ultimate goal of political reform away from monarchy and autocracy was to liberate the individual from the tyranny of the one or the few over the many. But they also warned of the equal and perhaps even greater danger of the tyranny of the majority over the minority or even over the one. Their ideal was not unrestricted democracy but individual liberty under a constitutional order limiting the powers of the government.

When the classical liberal thinkers spoke of the sovereignty of the people, they meant that each individual should be sovereign over the affairs of his own life. This was the idea behind the American Revolution of 1776, when the signers of the Declaration of Independence declared all men equal in possessing certain unalienable rights, among them life, liberty, and the pursuit of happiness—and that the government formed should secure and protect these individual rights. Any meaningful conception of "human rights" must refer to the individual rights of distinct human beings. There is no "collective" man. There are only separate individuals who think, value, hope, dream, and have goals and purposes that guide their lives.

The classical liberals of the past also emphasized that freedom is never secure if people do not have the means of living their lives independently and sometimes in opposition to the political authority. That is one reason they considered the right to private property essential and crucial. Private property gives an individual ownership and control over a portion of the means of production through which he may choose how and for what purposes he will live his life. Private property gives him a "territory" that is under his own jurisdiction, a degree of self-rule, in his home and on his property. In the free classical liberal society he can design his personal "country" to fit his values, ideals, and desires.

It is true that no man is an island. Man is a social animal who needs the assistance and companionship of his fellow men. In that free classical liberal society human association is brought about through the market and its social system of division of labor. The advantage of the market economy is that an individual can choose and find his niche in the nexus of voluntary exchange to acquire those things that will enable him to fulfill his own vision of the good life and its purposes.

This will not come without a cost. To earn the income that permits him, as a consumer, to buy the things that will enable him to live that unconventional life may require him to work at tasks he finds irksome or unattractive. On the other hand, he can choose to earn a living doing something he enjoys, but he may have to forgo the higher income possible had he chosen to produce and supply something potential customers might value more highly.

The market economy also offers the individual a degree of anonymity that helps shield him from the prying eyes and imposed values of others. Rarely do consumers of the multitudes of market-supplied goods and services know or care about the values, beliefs, or lifestyles of those who bring the demanded commodities to the buying public. A person making a product can earn a living and finance his personal vision of the good life even when many buyers of his product would, perhaps, radically disapprove of the way he leads his life with the income he has earned serving their wants.

The moral premise of the market is that men are prohibited from using either force or fraud in their dealings with each other. Each man's freedom to live and choose is respected by the others in the society, just as he is expected to respect their freedom in turn. Since coercion is prohibited in the market, if a man wishes the companionship or cooperation of other people he must learn to practice courtesy, honesty, and trustworthiness in all his dealings with them. Otherwise they will turn from him and associate and do business with others who are more respectful and sensitive in their dealings. Thus, the fact that all interactions in the market are voluntary and based on mutual consent results in men becoming more civil and refined in their relationships.

Furthermore, the marketplace is far more democratic than the political arena. In the free market each individual makes his own decisions concerning a variety of tradable goods and services. Given his preferences and his wealth and income, he purchases the combination of goods and services that he thinks will most enhance the quality, enjoyment, and purpose of his life. In the private free market, his decisions do not directly restrict the decisions of others. That one man enjoys ham and eggs for breakfast does not prevent another from buying cold cereal for his morning meal, and still a third from choosing to buy nothing at all to eat and instead spending his money some other way.

The entrepreneurs and businessmen on the supply side of the market respond to our different demands by competing against each other for the purchase and hire of the resources, capital equipment, and labor services with which the goods can be produced. Entrepreneurs and businessmen cannot compel consumers to purchase the goods and services they bring to market. They must persuade the buying public on the basis of the qualities and prices of the goods they offer for sale. Nor can they force people to work for them as suppliers of resources and labor services. Each entrepreneur and businessman competes against his rivals for the purchase, renting, or hire of those resource owners and workers. And neither are any of those entrepreneurs and businessmen guaranteed to make a profit, or even to break even, unless the consumers choose to purchase what is offered for sale.

What gets produced and the prices at which those goods are sold ultimately are determined by the public who "vote" with their money. At the same time, the outcomes of the market are "pluralistic." That is, the market provides a form of "proportional representation." Minorities are supplied with goods and services as is the majority, and to the degree that reflects the spending of their money "votes" in the market. Indeed, any minority of consumers can receive at least some of the goods and services they desire as long as they are willing and able to offer prices for them sufficient to cover the costs of a supplier bringing those goods to market.

But don't consumers in the market have an unequal number of "votes" in terms of the amount of money incomes they have with which to demand the various goods they desire? Yes, that is true. But in a free competitive market, the number of money "votes" each consumer has is a reflection of the income he has earned as a producer supplying other goods that his fellow consumers wished to buy. Thus each individual's relative income share in society is a reflection of what other members of the society think his services are worth.

The Political Process and the Bureaucratic Dilemma

The democratic pluralism of the free market economy stands in stark contrast to the outcome that results from the political democratic process. The goods and services provided by government are not open to individual decisionmaking and choice. We cannot pick and choose among the government goods and services in terms of the relative amounts we would like to have. And we certainly cannot choose to completely reject some of those goods and services and not have them at all. Nor do we have the option to pay only for the government goods and services we do want. Government acquires the financial means to supply the things it supplies to society through taxation, the compulsory taking of a part of the citizenry's income and wealth without their individual voluntary consent.

In a dictatorship this taking is determined by the wishes of the ruler and those closest to him on the basis of their needs and uses for the resources of the nation. In the democratic society, the limits on taxation are dependent on the extent to which those in political power are able to persuade the general population that the forced taking through taxation is a legitimate reflection of "the people's" own will as expressed in the electoral process. It is also influenced by the formation of coalitions of special interest groups that participate in justifying and pressuring for various government programs, for redistributing income and restricting markets through regulation, trade barriers, and monopoly privileges. These are all claimed, of course, to be in the "national interest" or for the "common good."

Nowhere is the difference and distinction between the market and the government as great as in matters of national defense and foreign policy, which are, by definition, socialist enterprises. They are monopolized and "owned" by the government. Private competition is legally prohibited and there are no market prices for actions undertaken and services rendered that allow individual members of the society to vote for or against such actions with their pocketbooks.

To change the course of national defense and foreign policy strategies and activities requires changing the elected representatives and the political parties in office that represent particular ideologies and philosophies concerning the role and responsibilities of government in society. The individual who wishes to see a change in national defense and foreign policy must persuade a large number of his fellow citizens to see things as he does and then get them to care enough about such a change to vote the incumbent politicians and parties out of office. And he only gets to attempt this every few years, depending on the electoral cycle of the democratic system under which he lives.

The problems with government "production" and "supplying" of any good or service is well illustrated by the new cabinet-level Department of Homeland Security that President George W. Bush first proposed during a nationwide television address on the evening of June 6, 2002. The president stated that "America is leading the civilized world in a titanic struggle against terror. Freedom and fear are at war. And freedom is winning." But in this war it is necessary to increase our vigilance, he said, and be even more on our guard against potential terrorist attacks directed at the territory of the United States. Toward this end President Bush assured us that "We're taking significant steps to strengthen our homeland protections: securing cockpits, tightening our borders, stockpiling vaccines, increasing security at water treatment and nuclear power plants."

But the president argued that more was required. He asked Congress to join him "in creating a single, permanent department with an overriding and urgent mission: securing the homeland of America and protecting the American people. . . . I propose a permanent Cabinet-level Department of Homeland Security to unite essential agencies that must work more closely together—among them the Coast Guard, the Border Patrol, the Customs Service, immigration officials, the Transportation Security Administration, and the Federal Emergency Management Agency. Employees of this new agency will come to work every morning knowing their most important job is to protect their fellow citizens."

In all the president called for combining 22 federal agencies into the new Homeland Security department, with an initial budget of $37.5 billion and a workforce of almost 170,000 federal employees. The president specified the tasks for which the new department would be responsible. It would control U.S. borders and prevent and interdict terrorists and their weapons from entering the country. It would work with and coordinate state and local governments for quick responses to emergency situations. It would employ and contract with "our best scientists" to develop methods of detecting biological, chemical, and nuclear weapons, as well as drugs and treatments to protect the American people from such weapons of mass destruction.

The Department of Homeland Security would also review and integrate intelligence and law enforcement data from a variety of other federal agencies, including the Federal Bureau of Investigation (FBI) and the Central Intelligence Agency (CIA). The purpose, the president said, would be to "produce a single daily picture of threats against our homeland. Analysts will be responsible for imagining the worst and planning to counter it."

At the same time, he assured the American people that this did not involve any additional growth in the size of government. "The staff of this new department will be largely drawn from the agencies we are combining." Indeed, he suggested that the U. S taxpayer could even expect cost savings. "By ending duplication and overlap, we will spend less on overhead and more on protecting America."

The fact is that President Bush's proposal represents one of the greatest concentrations of power and control within one federal agency created in the last half-century. The guiding purpose is to prevent terrorist attacks reaching American shores. Everything that the Department of Homeland Security is to do is to be focused on that one primary mission. All of its authority, all of its jurisdictional responsibilities will be judged and directed in pursuit of that goal.

Over time, as always happens with new government agencies, the department head will come to the Congress, year after year, claiming that the department has served the nation well in fulfilling its task. But he will insist that the department needs even more funds, a larger workforce, and an enlarged mandate of jurisdiction and power if it is to hold back the terrorist barbarians at the gate and keep the American people safe and secure. He will warn of cracks in the wall that only can be sealed if the department and other security-related agencies have even more latitude to encroach, intrude, and intervene in the private, personal, and commercial affairs of the American public.

In other words, its mission will never be completed, the terrorist threat will never be defeated, and the justification for the department's existence will never reach its end. Economists who have developed the "public choice" approach to analyzing the political arena have effectively demonstrated that the reason for this can be found in the motives of those who come to man the bureaucracy and those who financially benefit from its continuing existence.[1] Fighting this declared war on terrorism will become the "rice bowl" of those employed within the branches of the Department of Homeland Security. Their "daily bread" will now be dependent upon showing that they are doing their job and that their job is never finished. The department's expansion, both in terms of budget and responsibility, becomes the avenue within the organization for promotion and higher incomes. This becomes their "niche" in the division of labor upon which their livelihood is dependent. Winning the war on terrorism would mean the unemployment line—or worse, a job in the profit-oriented private sector.

At the same time, an array of private sector companies and corporations will see their own financial futures linked to the size and budget of the department. These will be the private enterprises that receive the contracts and supply the goods and services that the various branches of the department will need: from the companies that sell pens and paperclips all the way to the suppliers of high-tech surveillance and monitoring equipment. The latter, for example, will see economic benefit with every increase in the department's authority to snoop and pry into the private lives of Americans.

It is also worth keeping in mind that the new department will bring together within its jurisdiction a large number of experts in surveillance and investigative work. In other words, they are people who like doing what they do. Back in the 1930s, Chicago economist Frank H. Knight pointed out that "the probability of the people in power being individuals who would dislike the possession and exercise of power is on a level with the probability that an extremely tender-hearted person would get the job of whipping-master in a slave plantation."[2] Those who will have power and responsibility in the Department of Homeland Security are not likely to suffer long, sleepless nights deeply worried that they might have violated some innocent citizen's privacy and personal freedoms that day. More likely many of them will wonder how they can get around whatever legal restrictions and prohibitions seem to stand in the way of "getting the job done."

Furthermore, there will be no way of knowing whether the Department of Homeland Security is doing its job. Has the department spent too little or too much on infiltrating suspected terrorist organizations? Should more men and money be devoted to airport security or to developing antichemical warfare vaccines? If no "dirty nukes" are set off within the United States but two suicide bombers blow themselves up in congested urban areas during the lunch hour, killing and injuring hundreds of people, has the Department succeeded or failed in its mission? Will the people of America be better off if their taxes go up by some increment to increase the department's counterterrorist activities, which means they have less to spend on retirement investment accounts, their children's education, starting up or expanding a small business, or going on that dream vacation? If no terrorist attacks occur within the United States, does this prove that every dollar spent on the department's activities was well spent?

There can be no answers to any of these questions. Austrian economist Ludwig von Mises explained the reason for this during the Second World War in *Bureaucracy*, a small book he published in 1944.[3] He contrasted the inherent and inescapable difference between the profit-oriented management of an enterprise and the bureaucratical management of a government agency.

In the competitive free market, success or failure is determined and measured by the degree to which any private enterprise has either earned profits or suffered losses. Every current expense or capital outlay is estimated and compared with the margin of extra profit the expenditures and investments are expected to bring forth. If it is anticipated that the additional costs will be greater than the potential additional earnings from sales of a product or service to the consuming public the expenditures are not undertaken. If the outlays and investments are undertaken, the expectations that have made them seem worthwhile are eventually confronted with reality when more or better products come onto the market for sale and the earned additional revenues are either greater or smaller than the extra costs incurred.

In addition, Mises explained, no matter how large an enterprise or corporation may become, its branches and departments can be given a wide latitude of responsibility and decisionmaking yet still be controlled and coordinated with other parts of the enterprise through the profit and loss statements of the various divisions of the company. Those departments and branches suffering losses or earning relatively smaller profits may be reduced in size and activity if it is believed that product innovation or marketing or a dif-ferent manager would not result in their realizing a better return. On the other hand, those branches experiencing relatively higher profits may receive more resources and investments if their profit opportunities seem likely to continue.

Market prices reflect both consumer demand for a good and the scarcity of resources, labor, and capital employable in alternative lines of production. Profit and loss expectations and outcomes demonstrate relative success and failure both within and among firms and enterprises. Together they act as the steering mechanism that guides the use of resources and manpower to reflect the changing patterns of market demand and supply. They give rationality, order, and direction to the arenas of production and exchange.[4]

Government departments, bureaus, agencies, and enterprises operate and function in an entirely different way. Government may have to purchase all the goods and services and resources with which to run its various activities in the marketplace, but it raises the money to buy these things through taxation, not through the sale of a product to willing consumers in the marketplace. Neither does government supply its "products" and "services" to the citizenry at market price. The government supplies them "free" or at an arbitrary price that does not in any way reflect a "real" market value.

In addition, profitability is not the standard by which the actions and outcomes of government departments are judged. In the private sector, individuals decide how much personal security to invest in when they purchase locks and bolts for their doors, bars for their windows, and alarm systems for their homes and businesses. Consumer demand generates market prices that determine profitability and thus guide the investment of resources in private enterprises supplying these goods.

But the activities of government departments, bureaus, and enterprises cannot be evaluated, judged, and supervised by profit-and-loss balance sheets. Their activities and standards of success or failure are outside the market. The only way to determine that these branches of government are fulfilling the goals and targets that validate their existence is to set up "rules" and "procedures" that specify how those working in the bureaucracy are expected to perform. This is the method by which those employed in government are made accountable for what they do and how much they spend.

It doesn't matter how "irrational" or "terrifying" a bureaucrat's behavior may seem. In bureaucracy, the rule is not that the "customer is always right," but whether the proper forms have been completed in the correct sequence. Success is not measured by whether a new and better product has been manufactured, sold, and earned a profit, indicating enhanced consumer satisfaction. Success is measured by following "procedures" and "rules," regardless of whether doing so harms the tax-paying public.[5]

The expansion or contraction of some subdivision of a government agency is not guided by profit or loss. Instead, political fashions, fads, and "crises" usually provide the rationales and justifications for larger budgets, increased manpower, and greater authority over some segment of social and economic life.

On June 7, the day after President Bush's speech calling for the creation of the Department of Homeland Security, an article appeared on the editorial page of *The Wall Street Journal* titled "The FBI and CIA are First of All Bureaucracies," written by Daniel Henninger, one of the paper's deputy editors. He pointed out that "above all else these two agencies are bureaucracies. Worse still, they are large political bureaucracies." He referred to "the numbing, incentive-killing, rule-laden reality of life in the hallways [of these two organizations] for thousands of agents," and said that the FBI and CIA have had "perverse procedures, maladjusted incentives and political obeisances no different than the IRS, the FAA, HCFA, the United Nations, the Vatican, or the local hospital or the INS." He suggested, "It's time for Washington to find a way to a 'Post-Bureaucratic Society.'" What these and other bureaucracies need, Henninger suggested, is a good shakeup with businesslike management under the supervision of some successful corporate executive to get things in hand and on the right track.[6]

In his 1944 book *Bureaucracy*, Mises had already given the answer to this suggestion. An enterprise or activity is either guided by the pursuit of profit or it is not: Make profits by satisfying consumers better than the market supply-side rivals or meet the legislative mandate of the bureau or agency by following the rules and procedures specified in your job description. Those who head government departments, bureaus, and agencies are answerable and responsive to politicians, interest groups, and the changing political currents and crises that influence public policy. Success is measured by bigger budgets and increased power, fueled by never-ending "social problems" that justify the bureaucracy's existence.[7]

A new Department of Homeland Security guarantees, therefore, that America will very likely have a war on terrorism for decades to come—whether "objectively" the terrorist threat has been radically reduced or eliminated. It assures that constant pressure will be applied to ensure that the department has more control and the latitude to interfere in the lives of the ordinary American citizen. It makes certain that no matter how few or how many terrorist attacks may be perpetrated within the borders of the United States in the coming years, it will demonstrate what a fine job the department has been doing and what a better job it could do if only it had more money and power. And there will be no market-equivalent test or standard to measure its successes or failures because it will be operating, like all government activities, outside the arena of competitive supply and demand.

This is not meant to challenge the legitimacy of the idea that society needs a government that has as its purpose the securing and protecting of the rights to life, liberty, and property. But it is useful to remind ourselves of the fundamental and unbridgeable differences between the market institutions of individual choice and freedom and the political regime of monopoly government control and coercion.

The Market Economy and
Government Regulatory Interventions

A similar problem arises from government intervention in the market. In the free market, as we have seen, the only way for the successful entrepreneur to earn profits and avoid losses is to direct the resources under his ownership and control into making those products for which he believes consumers are willing to pay a price above the costs of production. The prices for resources, labor, and capital that have been competitively formed on the market enable him to undertake the process of economic calculation. He determines which of the technologically possible ways of combining those factors of production to make his product is the least-cost way.

But the entrepreneur does more than merely passively take those market prices as "givens." He also imagines and implements new methods of production. He devises ways to make goods at lower costs and with improved qualities. He creates new products that he anticipates consumers will find attractive. The qualities of a truly successful and forward-looking entrepreneur were described by Austrian economist Friedrich von Wieser:

> It is customary to attribute the merits of economic progress to the discoveries and inventions of modern technical science without giving special thought to the entrepreneur. In reality, technical progress could never be realized without the great entrepreneur. By organizing his enterprise, he also acts as a discoverer and inventor. He resembles a social dowser in the scent that he has for how to get hold of the varied complementary factors that the modern capitalistic enterprise has to combine and for the turns that supply and demand will take. In addition, the great entrepreneur must be a strong-willed man . . . who conjures up salaried and wage employees and trains them for their jobs. It takes a strong, untiring effort to think through in every detail and to put into practice the entrepreneurial concept which corresponds to a given state of technical knowledge and to a given market situation. The subsequent entrepreneurs who copy the new model don't have to be such dominating types any more as were the innovating first entrepreneurs. Yet the rapidly changing technical and market conditions of our time keep posing ever new tasks calling for the great entrepreneur. . . . [T]he great entrepreneur needs a free mind and an unfettered will in order to live up to the

constantly changing requirements of the time. The doctrine of individualism expounded by the classical economists is tailored to fit the person of the modern entrepreneur. . . . When classical doctrine demanded freedom for the economy it fundamentally meant the freedom, the right of self-determination, of the entrepreneur.[8]

And all of his efforts are geared toward that end-point task of satisfying the demands of the consuming public better than his competition. Every change in the underlying circumstances and conditions of market supply and demand brings about new constraints and new opportunities which each entrepreneur must adjust to and take advantage of—if he is to continue to earn profits and not suffer losses.

The role of competition in the market is to provide the incentive and the avenue for each of those responsible for a business enterprise to have the motive to adapt and improve. And in doing so they configure and conform the direction of production, the allocation of resources, and the distribution of earned income among those participating in the production process.

Government interventionist policies distort and deter this market process. First, as was once pointed out, "Prices must be completely free, if they are to tell the truth."[9] Protectionist tariffs, minimum wages, farm price supports (to name just a few that most people are familiar with) raise, set, or guarantee prices in the marketplace differently than those prices formed exclusively by the competitive forces of supply and demand. As a consequence they distort the information and the incentives guiding private enterprises into producing various products or hiring various quantities of different factors of production. The wrong products are produced with the wrong uses and combinations of resources. Waste, inefficiency, and imbalances between supply and demand inevitably follow from the government making prices different from "the truth" that would have resulted from the private and interacting choices of market participants.[10]

Government interventions regulating production methods and techniques are no less disruptive of the market process. Rules, restrictions, and requirements imposed on the methods and techniques by which enterprises may manufacture goods and employ the factors of production invariably, by definition, represent ways of making products differently than if these decisions were made by responsible entrepreneurs and enterprise managers.

But must not such rules, restrictions, and requirements be imposed on private enterprise to assure the necessary product safety and quality for the consumer and a reasonable workplace environment for those employed within private business?

Forty years ago, free market economist and Nobel Laureate Milton Friedman published a short book titled *Capitalism and Freedom*.[11] One chapter was devoted to occupational licensure by government. Friedman explained the various anticompetitive results caused by regulatory restrictions on the freedom of occupation and profession in the marketplace. He pointed out that occupational licensing served as an important political vehicle for professional groups to limit entry into various types of employment, and thus acted as a strong pro-monopoly policy in society.

Friedman also argued that government enforcement of or support for licensing standards and rules for entering and practicing a particular profession or skilled occupation also limited innovation, change, and improvement by requiring practitioners to follow "approved" methods and techniques in providing services to the consuming public. In place of government licensing, Friedman suggested that a market left free and unregulated would develop (as it had in the past) market methods for providing both information to the buying public and rules and standards for assuring the quality and reliability of goods and services sold to consumers. The market solution to product safety and service quality was voluntary private certification, which market producers and suppliers have profit incentives to enter into and follow in marketing their products. He explained:

> There are private certification agencies in many areas that certify the competence of a person or the quality of a particular product. The Good Housekeeping seal is a private certification arrangement. For industrial products there are private testing

laboratories that will certify to the quality of a particular product. For consumer products, there are consuming testing agencies of which Consumers Union and Consumers' Research are the best known in the United States. Better Business Bureaus are voluntary organizations that certify the quality of particular dealers. Technical schools, colleges and universities certify the quality of their graduates. One function of retailers . . . is to certify the quality of the many items they sell. The consumer develops confidence in the store, and the store in turn has an incentive to earn this confidence by investigating the quality of the items it sells.[12]

More recently, in *Regulation without the State . . . The Debate Continues*, John Blundell and Colin Robinson have taken up this same argument and have developed it with great cogency.[13] They begin their case for removing government from economic regulation by carefully explaining the numerous negative effects of government intervention. First, the advocates of regulation assume that the regulators possess the knowledge and ability to successfully evaluate standards and changing circumstances in the market, which is very far from the case.

Second, the costs of government regulation are often hidden and not merely because of the cost of running the bureaucracies responsible for enforcing the regulations, but also because of the private sector's expenses of complying with the rules and controls. The full costs make it far from certain that, even on a basic cost-benefit basis, the gains from such regulations could be rationalized as worth the financial burden on the society.

Third, those who impose the regulations—the regulators in the government bureaucracies—bear none of the direct costs, burdens, or inconveniences, and therefore have no incentive to limit the number or the extent of the regulatory expenses they impose on others. Hence, regulation tends to run amok over time.

Fourth, special interest groups have strong incentives to lobby for market regulation as a means to limit competition and new entrants and to control and capture greater control over their particular markets.

Blundell and Robinson point out that "regulation" means the establishment of rules. "Rules are an essential part of life," they say. "But making them is not necessarily a government function; they can be (and usually are) established through voluntary action. . . . Contrary to conventional wisdom, the alternative to state regulation is not a regulatory void, but a range of voluntary arrangements."[14]

As an example they refer to Underwriters Laboratories (UL) in the United States, which supplies private and voluntary certification for such products as electrical appliances, automotive products, medical appliances, alarm systems, and chemicals. Indeed, they point out that one reason a private certification association such as UL has to maintain the quality and reliability of its testing methods and standards is that it operates in a competitive field of 12 other certification associations, each interested in gaining and maintaining trust from their members and the general public.

The authors also observe that there are private organizations such as Green Seal and Eco-Rating that supply private certification concerning the "environmental-friendly" qualities of products, for those in society for whom this matters. And like Friedman 40 years ago, they refer to the Good Housekeeping Institute and *Consumer Reports* as private organizations that provide both stamps of approval and information concerning the quality of products and the promises made by their manufacturers about them.

Nor are such private associations for standards and reliability in product marketing a new phenomenon. Blundell and Robinson tell the story of the development of the steam-boiler assurance industry in the nineteenth century. The new steam boilers introduced to British industry in the middle of the 1800s often experienced failures and explosions, causing major damage and injury. Engineers, scientists, manufacturers, and mill owners formed an association for research and sharing knowledge on how to better construct, install, and operate steam boilers. In the late 1850s and 1860s, this led to the establishment of a group of insurance companies in this industry that organized testing and examination of steam boilers as a basis for providing insurance policies. The insurance companies also fostered research in innovations to make steam boilers safer and more efficient.

Rent-Seeking in the Political Process

The political process disrupts the market economy and entrepreneurial activity in another way, known in the economic literature as "rent-seeking." This is a misnomer because what is actually meant is the pursuit of profits through the political process rather than in the market arena. Thus, it more appropriately should be called *political profit-seeking*, as opposed to market profit-seeking.

The starting point of public choice theory, out of which the theory of rent-seeking has developed, is that the logic and rationality of the political process has the same foundation as economic theory in general. Individuals, whether in the marketplace or the political arena, are guided by self-interested motives to improve their circumstances: They weigh costs and benefits, and they respond to incentives.

As in the marketplace, there are demanders in politics—those who desire favors and privileges from the government; and there are suppliers—politicians who offer favors and privileges in return for campaign contributions and votes. In addition, there are the bureaucratic managers of the regulatory, interventionist, and redistributive system, who are constantly on the lookout for ways and means to expand their authority and increase their budgets as avenues to more power and opportunities for promotion and higher salaries.

Why do voters not see through the propagandistic smoke screen that is used to rationalize this process of legalized plunder? It is because voters are "rationally ignorant." For any one voter, his ballot, in terms of its potential to make the difference in any election, is insignificant in relation to all the votes cast. For most people it is just not worth the personal cost in time and expense to become intelligently informed on all the various policy issues that are being advocated by politicians, interest groups, and bureaucrats.

What motivates the drive for government favors and privileges is "rent-seeking" behavior.[15] In the free marketplace, the only way in which producers can earn revenues and profits is by successfully competing against their rivals in offering better and less expensive goods to the consuming public. But, there is another route to profits: the use of government to obtain restrictions and protections limiting the ability of market rivals to compete, or to receive direct government subsidies or contracts from the government to gain profits.

The costs from this process of politically acquired profits are the resources and labor devoted to manipulating the political process to one's advantage rather than to producing the goods and services potentially desired by consumers. Furthermore, successful rent seeking results in closed-off markets and limits on competition, which in the longer run reduce the innovation and competitive rivalry that normally act as the stimulus for improvements in the quantities, varieties, and prices of goods available.

In this interventionist state of privilege and favor, in which there is now the pursuit of politically based profits, the entrepreneurial process is distorted in another way. The businessman must now undertake expenditures and hire personnel in the quest of profits in the political arena, which has nothing to do with normal market-based decisionmaking. In 1932, in the politically corrupted twilight of the German Weimar Republic shortly before Hitler came to power, Ludwig von Mises explained the perverse economic environment of the hyperinterventionist state:

> We . . . live in an interventionist state, in which every enterprise—and particularly large enterprises that are despised by demagogues and aristocrats alike—must be intent on currying and maintaining the favor of those in power so the government interventions can be in its benefit and not to its detriment. A business that wants to guard itself from destruction by interventionist policy must ingratiate itself both "above" and "below" and must take a myriad of issues into consideration that it would neglect under purely commercial conditions. This influences not only industrial relations but also all other aspects of management. One has to make an accommodation with government and local authorities, one has to allow for all prejudices and wishes of public opinion, one has to trim one's sails to the wind. One has to do obviously unprofitable business, contribute money to election funds and newspapers, employ friends of

government and of politicians, and dismiss those who have
fallen out of favor. One has to get on good terms with trade
unions and churches, support the arts and sciences, and be
"charitable." In a word, one has to incur all sorts of expenditure
for matters not related to one's business.[16]

The entrepreneur's economic calculations under such a situation are no longer solely guided or dictated by the logic of market
profit and loss. No longer does the entrepreneur weigh the hiring
of personnel on the basis of the expected value of their contributions to manufacturing, marketing, and selling a product or a service to prospective consumers. No longer does he merely evaluate
whether a possible expenditure, at the margin, will advance or
inhibit his attempts to make that better product at a lower cost, so
as to offer the good or service at more attractive terms than his
next closest rival who is also trying to win over consumers. Now he
has to deal with ephemeral expenses and employments outside the
normal setting of supply and demand. Mises explained the implications of this as well:

> Since the impact of these individual expenditures on business
> success cannot be measured in monetary terms, they throw the
> calculation of profitability severely into disarray. *How* is one to
> account for the benefits derived from governmental favors and
> other non-economic factors and balance them against the losses
> caused by an incompetent director who is well liked "above,"
> or by the employment of engineers agreeable to political
> parties instead of capable engineers? If former ministers of
> government and relatives and friends of active statesmen and
> politicians are appointed to the boards of companies, if public
> officials and members of respected clubs and organizations
> occupy positions of middle management, and if all workers
> are union members, the enterprise will necessarily perish. If it
> can keep its competitive position in spite of its bureaucratic
> nature, this can only be due to government intervention. But
> since it could not survive without intervention in its favor it is
> forced to become ever more bureaucratic.[17]

The reason Mises referred to this as a step toward "bureaucratization" of private enterprise is that the entrepreneur, the businessman, now has to be guided by decisionmaking principles not reducible to the same economic calculative process as practiced in the non-politicized free market. What cost or benefit weight do you assign to having, as Mises put it, an "incompetent director" on the company's board who "knows the right people," say, in the Department of Commerce, or who is on "good terms" with a lawyer who is working with an investigative team in the antitrust division of the Justice Department that is looking into possible "anticompetitive" conduct by your company? What weight do you give in such profit and loss calculations to the company's philanthropic giving to "the arts" because it puts one of the company's officers on a charity board with the wife of a Senator who is on an important congressional committee that sets tax, tariff, or regulatory policy?

The permutations of this process in the interventionist state is endless precisely because of the degree to which the government intrudes into virtually every aspect and detail of business and corporate activity. And to this extent, Mises was arguing, the decisionmaking, resource use, and monetary expenditures within the enterprise are outside the nexus of market supply and demand, in a manner similar to the government bureaucracy that operates on the basis of having nothing to do with serving or responding to consumer demand. It is certainly not to the same extreme as the bureaucratic agency or department precisely because the private enterprise still operates in a market in which it must offer a product or service consumers are interested in buying.[18]

Nonetheless, the politicization of the marketplace through government interventionist policies deflects the activities and market-oriented rationality of the entrepreneurial process. The businessman must now cater to the demands, interests, and pressures surrounding politicians and those who supervise and oversee the bureaucratic agencies whose legislative and regulatory decisions can influence, if not determine, the fate of a company. And in this way, private enterprise becomes enveloped in the spider's web of political intrigue and manipulation that is the inevitable result of the interventionist state.

Political Corruption and the
Interventionist State

While many see the problem, few see the solution. For example, in August 2002, Transparency International, a nongovernmental organization (NGO) headquartered in Berlin, Germany, released its *Corruption Perceptions Index* for 2002, which covers 102 countries. The index attempts to estimate, on a scale of zero to ten (with zero designating "highly corrupt" and 10 being "highly clean"), "the degree to which corruption is perceived to exist among public officials and politicians." The index "focuses on corruption in the public sector and defines corruption as the abuse of public office for private gain," meaning, for example, "bribe-taking by public officials in public procurement." It is based on various surveys meant to "garner the perceptions of both residents and expatriates, both business people and risk analysts," giving "a snapshot of the views of decisionmakers, who make key decisions on investment and trade."

Way at the bottom of the list, nearest that "highly corrupt" point of zero are, not surprisingly, a large number of countries in Asia and Africa and most of the former Soviet Republics. But while Finland is the "cleanest" with a rating of 9.7, with Denmark and New Zealand close seconds with 9.5, all the other countries of Western Europe and North America suffer from degrees of corruption according to Transparency International. The United States is listed number 16 with an index rating of 7.7.

Transparency International states in its summary of results that "[p]olitical elites and their cronies continue to take kickbacks at every opportunity. Hand and glove with corrupt business people, they are trapping whole nations in poverty and hampering sustainable development." So what is to be done? Transparency International, hailing itself as "the only global non-governmental and not-for-profit organization devoted solely to curbing corruption," concludes that "[d]eveloped countries have a special humanitarian responsibility given the resources as their disposal, to investigate and prosecute the companies within their jurisdictions that are bribing. Their bribes and incentives to corrupt public officials and politicians are subverting the orderly development of poor nations, already trapped, as they are, in a vicious circle of crippling poverty, hunger and disease."[19]

What Transparency International and many others around the world fail to understand is that their focus on prosecuting companies that pay bribes confuses the symptom for the disease. The reason bribery and corruption exist is precisely because governments have favors and privileges to hand out; it is because so much of social and economic life has been politicized. And certainly the degree to which this prevails is greatest in countries at the lower end of this corruption perception index. But wherever governments control production and marketing activities, either through outright ownership or heavy-handed regulation, those who politically supervise access within these sectors of the economy will see gains from trade with those who desire selective entrée to the profit opportunities offered. This will apply whether it pertains to being awarded a government procurement contract, receiving a differential tax break or subsidy, obtaining an anticompetitive regulation to one's special benefit, or a tariff barrier that wards off foreign rivals.

Restoring the Self-Governing Individual in the Free Marketplace

This is only one way to end this type of political corruption. It is the same way that rent-seeking activity can be eliminated. And it is the same way to redirect market entrepreneurs to their essential task of creatively and innovatively overseeing the use of the means of production for the fulfillment of the demands of the consuming public, which means everyone in society.

The interventionist state needs to be repealed. If this repeal were to be formulated as a new amendment to the United States Constitution, it might be phrased something like the following:

> Congress shall make no law abridging the peaceful and voluntary acquisition, use, or exchange of private property. No law or regulation shall be established interfering with private decisions concerning the peaceful and voluntary purchase, hire, and application of the means of production. Nor shall

any law or regulation be established setting or hindering the voluntary determination between buyers and sellers of the prices at which and the conditions under which all goods and services, including resources, land, capital, and labor, and financial and monetary instruments shall be bought and sold, hired, rented, or lent. Nor shall the government limit these freedoms to domestic transactions, but will allow the same free trading to exist between the citizens of the United States and the citizens of all other countries.

While I am sure a constitutional scholar would, no doubt, find some error or omission in the particular language I have used to articulate the idea, I think the concept is clear enough. What is needed is *a separation of market and state.* This would do away with the vast majority of potential temptations for political corruption. Why? Because then the government would no longer have the authority and power to bestow special privileges and favors on some at the expense of others in the marketplace. The only legal avenues open to all would be that peaceful and voluntary participation in the social system of division of labor, in which each individual must serve his fellow man through free exchange as the means to improve and further his own circumstances.

At the same time, and equally—if not more—important, the concept of individual self-government that was discussed at the beginning of this essay would not only be restored but greatly expanded. Each would be, to a far greater degree than now, a self-governing individual guided by his own purposes and plans, but by legal and moral obligation respectful of the equal right of every other man to have the same freedom. The plurality of the marketplace would once again triumph over the homogeneity of the political arena.

Also, the entire world would benefit, since the human mind and spirit, with their creative potential, would have been liberated from the confines and corruption of political uniformity and control. And out of this could come a new epoch, in a new century of liberty and prosperity, which would fulfill the hopes and dreams of those who founded our country and who conceived of the establishment of freedom for all men everywhere.

Notes

[1]James M. Buchanan and Robert D. Tollison, eds., *Theory of Public Choice: Political Applications of Economics* (Ann Arbor: University of Michigan, 1972); and *Theory of Public Choice—II* (Ann Arbor: University of Michigan, 1984); James M. Buchanan, et al., *The Economic of Politics* (London: Institute of Economic Affairs, 1978); Dennis C. Mueller, *Public Choice* (Cambridge: Cambridge University Press, 1979); and Gordon Tullock, et al., *Government: Whose Obedient Servant? A Primer in Public Choice* (London: Institute of Economic Affairs, 2000).

[2]Frank H. Knight, review of "Lippmann's 'The Good Society,'" *Journal of Political Economy* (December 1938): 869.

[3]Ludwig von Mises, *Bureaucracy* (New Haven, CT: Yale University Press, 1944).

[4]Ibid., pp. 20–39.

[5]Ibid., pp. 41–56.

[6]Daniel Henniger, "The FBI and CIA are First of All Bureaucracies," *The Wall Street Journal* (June 7, 2002): A22.

[7]Ibid., pp. 57–63; see also Ludwig von Mises, "Commerical and Bureaucratic Business Management" [1930] in Richard M. Ebeling, ed., *Selected Writings of Ludwig von Mises*, Vol. 2. *Between the Two World Wars: Monetary Disorder, Interventionism, Socialism, and the Great Depression* (Indianapolis, IN: Liberty Fund, 2002), p. 164: "It is an absolute and complete mistake to think that the 'commercial' is a form of organization that can simply be grafted onto the business of government in order to debureaucratize it. The reason is that public enterprises operate not merely to earn profits but to pursue other goals as well. That is precisely the reason why these enterprises are supposed to be in public hands. But if the achievement of goals other than the maximization of profits became central to the management of the enterprise, then profit maximization no longer guides the enterprise and bureaucratic methods are introduced."

[8]Friedrich von Wieser, *The Law of Power* [1926] (Lincoln, NE: Bureau of Business Research, 1983), pp. 347–48.

[9]F. A. Harper, "The Crisis of the Free Market" [1945], reprinted in *The Writings of F. A. Harper*, vol. 1 (Menlo Park, CA: Institute for Humane Studies, 1978), p. 54.

[10]On the effect of price controls on the market economy, see *Ludwig von Mises, Critique of Interventionism* [1929] (Irvington-on-Hudson, NY: Foundation for Economic Education, 1996), pp. 7–11 & 97–106; *Interventionism: An Economic Analysis* [1941] (Irvington-on-Hudson, NY: Foundation for Economic Education, 1998), pp. 23–34; *Human Action, A Treatise on Economics* (Irvington-on-Hudson, NY: Foundation for Economic Education, 4th revised ed., 1996), pp. 758–79; on the history of the consequences of price controls, see Robert L. Schuettinger and Eamonn F. Butler, *Forty Centuries*

of Wage and Price Controls (Washington, D.C.: Heritage Foundation, 1979); and Colin D. Campbell, ed., *Wage-Price Controls in World War II: United States and Germany* (Washington, D.C.: American Enterprise Institute, 1972).

[11]Milton Friedman, *Capitalism and Freedom* (Chicago: University of Chicago Press, 1962).

[12]Ibid., pp. 146–47.

[13]John Blundell and Colin Robinson, *Regulation Without the State... The Debate Continues* (London: Institute of Economic Affairs, 2000).

[14]Ibid., p. 1.

[15]James M. Buchanan, Robert D. Tollison, and Gordon Tullock, eds., *Toward a Theory of the Rent-Seeking Society* (College Station: Texas A & M University Press, 1980); David C. Colander, Ed., *Neoclassical Political Economy: The Analysis of Rent-Seeking and DUP Activities* (Cambridge, MA: Ballinger Publishing, 1984); Gordon Tullock, *The Economics of Special Privilege and Rent-Seeking* (Boston: Kluwer Academic Press, 1989); and Tullock, *Rent-Seeking* (Brookfield, VT: Edward Elgar, 1993).

[16]Ludwig von Mises, "Economic Calculation under Commercial Management and Bureaucratic Administration" [1932] in Richard M. Ebeling, ed., *Selected Writings of Ludwig von Mises*, Vol. 2. *Between the Two World Wars: Monetary Disorder, Interventionism, Socialism, and the Great Depression*, p. 378.

[17]Ibid., pp. 378–79.

[18]Mises, *Bureaucracy*, pp. 65–73.

[19]Transparency International, <www.transparency.org>, *Corruption Perceptions Index 2002*.

MICHAEL W. LYNCH

Welfare Policy Yesterday, Today, and Tomorrow

What does "welfare" mean? The strictest definition would be that it is a federal cash benefits program, formerly known as Aid to Families with Dependent Children (AFDC) and now called Temporary Assistance for Needy Families (TANF). This name change is instructive, and points to a major goal of the 1996 reform: to make welfare temporary. But a better working definition of welfare—and the one most often employed—accounts for myriad programs that assist low-income Americans with material needs. Called the "safety net" by bureaucrats and intellectuals and "the system" by those who rely on it, it includes TANF, Medicaid, HUD, SSI, childcare assistance, and food stamps. Some would even include the Earned Income Tax Credit, a program that sends cash to low-income workers as a tax refund. Currently governments spend roughly $328 billion a year on these programs. As a point of reference, the federal government spent $291 billion on national defense in 2001.

It is important to keep two things in mind when thinking about welfare in the United States. The many twists and turns in welfare policy since the nation's founding can be categorized into one of two types: structural shifts and philosophical shifts. The latter is what people think welfare ought to do. The former is how the system is designed and operated to accomplish its goals. These changes don't necessarily occur at the same time: The philosophical changes came in the 1930s and the 1960s; the most significant structural changes came in the 1930s and most recently in 1996. That this last change

is less revolutionary conceptually than practically does not necessarily bode well for the future.

Welfare Policy Yesterday

To frame this discussion in terms of the free market versus bureaucracy, today's welfare programs rely on bureaucracy, not the free
market. They are quintessential government redistribution programs, where, in the words of social scientist Charles Murray, whose
groundbreaking 1984 book, *Losing Ground*, provides much of the
historical information for these remarks, governments "take tax
dollars from one worker whose paycheck, the government has decided, is too large, and give them to another worker whose paycheck,
the government has decided, is too small."[1] The market certainly
provides all of these goods, and does so far better than bureaucrats.
Just compare private housing to public housing, private health
insurance to Medicaid, and so on. But can it do so for free?

The answer is that charity once did, but certainly not at the
levels we see today. Prior to the New Deal, when social security,
AFDC, Workman's Compensation, and unemployment insurance
came to life, people who fell on hard times had to rely on private
provisions or charity. Private provisions often took the form of
mutual aid societies, common in urban immigrant communities,
where people formed social clubs that also provided forms of social
insurance. Religious and other social reform groups, which tended
to be judgmental and distinguish between the deserving and undeserving poor, provided charity. Some states offered widow's pen-
sions and operated poorhouses.

There is a well-known, long-studied, and insoluble problem
with charity of any kind. Known as "The Samaritan's Dilemma" or
"the moral hazard," today's pop psychology calls it "enabling." Put
simply, the dilemma is that the very act of helping people when
they fall on hard times makes it more likely that they will indeed
fall on hard times. In economic terms, assistance lowers the costs of
being poor, makes it less unpleasant, and therefore more common.
This problem cannot be solved, only addressed, and some forms of

assistance address it better than others. Private groups, whose members often came from the communities they served, were able to distinguish between the deserving and undeserving poor, the former being widows or victims of a recession, the latter being ne'er-do-wells, drunks being a prime example.

But this is tricky and brings to mind Frank McCourt's novel *Angela's Ashes*. The husband was certainly a member of the undeserving poor. His family lived in wretched conditions, yet when he quit complaining about capitalism long enough to get a job, he proceeded to drink his wages. His wife and children, the deserving poor, never benefited.

The philosophical shift from private to public responsibility for the welfare of the deserving poor began when the government stepped in during the Depression and started providing social services. Each federal program targeted a specific segment of the needy. AFDC was designed to assist widows. Social security was to provide for the elderly who, after a lifetime of labor, were unable to work any longer. (At the time, most people didn't live long enough to collect any money.) Workman's compensation was geared to help injured workers; unemployment insurance was for those affected by the vagaries of the business cycle (not those who quit or were fired). The philosophical shift came with the acceptance of government— more specifically, the federal government—as the legitimate provider of such social insurance.

In the 1960s, President Lyndon Johnson's "War on Poverty" offered "A Hand, Not a Handout." It wasn't long, however, before the zeitgeist shifted, and the government was offering a series of handouts. Structural poverty became the buzzword, the idea that it wasn't the individual's fault that he or she was poor and couldn't find a job. It was the system's fault. People wanted to work; there just wasn't the opportunity. "What emerged in the mid-1960s," writes Murray, "was almost unbroken intellectual consensus that the individualist explanation of poverty was altogether outmoded and reactionary." "Poverty" he stated, "was not a consequence of indolence and vice. It was not the just desserts of people who didn't try hard enough. It was produced by conditions that had nothing to do with individual virtue or effort. Poverty was not the fault of the individual but of the system."[2] This philosophical shift led to a host of programs, most notably job training, long-term education subsidies, and community development efforts. The problem with these programs was that none of them worked.

That is not to say that they didn't work for anyone. These programs were quite generous and many people took advantage of them. Eloise Anderson, who helped former Wisconsin Governor Tommy Thompson develop the Badger State's innovative welfare reform effort before moving to California to direct that state's massive social services bureaucracy, briefly accepted government assistance. When her husband left her in 1973 with a small child, she signed up for food stamps. (I must add that she declared on *60 Minutes*, "I don't understand finding it too hard to work"; she pumped gas rather than accept the cash grant.) Welfare programs often provided support for women during such involuntary life transitions.

In Camden, New Jersey (a city we will discuss in some detail later), Cynthia Jordan Hannah, known as "Blondie," spoke approvingly of the old system and how it helped launch her career in social services. She went on welfare in 1975 when she had a baby. "They offered me a good package," she said.[3] Indeed, she was able to keep her food stamps, welfare check, and Medicaid while she studied for three years. After graduation she went to work for the government and to this day lives in public housing. There are thousands of similar stories.

Over time two distinct populations of welfare users developed: those for whom it was a short-term transition step, and those for whom it was a way of life. Usage statistics reflected this. Nearly one in three single parent recipients of welfare signed up for fewer than two years over their entire life. Yet the average time, the mean, spent on welfare was 6.5 years; over half spent more than five years on welfare.

Welfare Policy Today

In the 1990s America had a large welfare system, one based on the idea that not only was it the government's responsibility to prevent individuals from slipping into poverty, but that it was the government's fault that they were poor in the first place. Anyone who looked closely knew the programs were failures—and expensive failures at that. When Johnson embarked upon his War on Poverty, the Heritage Foundation's Robert Rector calculates that the federal government spent $42 billion in today's dollars on social welfare programs. Today, as we have seen, it spends more than seven times that amount. According to Rector, between 1965 and 2000 taxpayers shelled out $8.29 trillion in today's dollars for social welfare programs.[4] As a comparison, World War II, a genuine military effort, cost $3.3 trillion in today's dollars.

Some complained about the money, others were simply frustrated with the results. As Murray put it, "the problem was not how much it cost, but what it bought."[5] Enter President Clinton, a New Democrat, defined in part by his 1992 campaign promise to "End welfare as we know it." (This promise was nothing new. In 1964, as he signed a bill that would enable a huge expansion of the welfare state, then-President Lyndon Johnson promised that "the days of the dole in this country are numbered.")[6] But President Clinton ended up with something he wasn't expecting: A Republican Congress eager to help him keep his promise. He actually vetoed welfare reform legislation twice before signing the Personal Responsibility and Work Opportunity Reconciliation Act on August 22, 1996.

In many ways the act was quite a break from the past. It ended the welfare system's cash grant entitlement, which meant that no longer could anyone who met certain conditions be eligible for aid into perpetuity. Instead, it froze federal spending at its current level and block-granted the money to the states, many of which had already applied for waivers to experiment with their own programs. The act freed states to experiment, but with restrictions. Most notably, the states had to put a five-year time limit on the basic welfare grant funded by the federal government, and it ordered states to, for example, put half of their cash grant recipients to work within two years. It provided money for childcare grants, toughened child-support requirements, made immigrants ineligible for welfare, and funded a program to teach abstinence.

The reform, which was authorized for five years and is now up for reauthorization, was a synthesis of conservative and liberal ideas.

The aspect of the bill that received the most attention was the time limit, a conservative idea that focused the incentives on getting people off welfare. It is also true, but rarely mentioned because it serves no one's interest, that the new program spent far more money per person than had the old program. This resulted from both new grants—mostly childcare grants, but also various rewards for good performance—and the fact that federal funding stayed the same while caseloads dropped.

As we shall see, the 1996 Act reflected a shift in the structure of the program, which was to direct efforts toward mitigating the Samaritan's dilemma. But it didn't fully repudiate the idea that the federal government ought to provide for security. It certainly didn't undermine the idea that governments ought to supplement the earnings of low-income Americans.

Nevertheless, the break was too much for long-time liberals in Washington, D.C., to stomach, and their predictions were dire. Before the bill passed, the left-of-center Urban Institute produced a study showing that it would cast 2.6 million Americans—including 1.1 million children—into poverty. Homeless shelters, advocates for the poor predicted, would be overwhelmed. Soup kitchens wouldn't be able to cook enough stew to feed all the newly hungry. Two Clinton administration bigwigs quit in protest—and were widely hailed for their courage and principles. Said Daniel Patrick Moynihan, then a Democratic Senator, "We are putting our children at risk with absolutely no evidence that this radical idea has even the slightest chance of success."[7]

What happened? As of June 2001, 6 million Americans had left the welfare rolls—a rate of 6,000 a day at one point—bypassing the homeless shelters and soup kitchens on their way to work. States did not slash services as predicted, but experimented with new programs to support work. As their welfare rolls dropped, they pumped more money into programs such as childcare and transportation assistance. A rural county in New Jersey helps people purchase cars to get to work. West Virginia helps mothers purchase back-to-school clothes. In 1997, 70 percent of state welfare dollars went to cash grants, while 20 percent went to support programs. Today, 70 percent goes to support programs.

And what about poverty? As of 2000, the last year for which data is available, 5.4 million fewer Americans, 2.8 million fewer children, lived in poverty. By traditional measures—that is, the number of people on the rolls and the number of people living in poverty—the 1996 reforms can only be considered a smashing success.

But how has the program affected people's lives? I traveled to Camden, New Jersey, in the winter of 2000 to get a ground-level reading of welfare reform, how it was working—if it was working—in an urban setting. In the four days I spent there talking with welfare administrators, community activists, and current and former welfare recipients, I gained much insight into the 1996 reform, as well as into the old system. And I found out why the former is preferable. Camden is an old industrial town, right across the Delaware River from Philadelphia. It was once known for its shipyards, RCA plants, and Campbell Soup factories; today it is known mostly for sending three mayors in a row to prison and as a great place to buy crack and heroin. Its population peaked at 150,000. Only 83,000 people call it home today. It is a place so poor that cigarettes—an affordable luxury—are sold one at a time. Drug dealers, whose names are known to residents, reportedly buy blocks of boarded-up row houses so they can post effective lookouts. It has two employment centers—the county and city governments and the hospitals. Other than that, there are a few small businesses and a lot of abandoned buildings.

What I discovered in Camden surprised me. The new law is tremendously effective on the individual level, changing the way people think of welfare and hence their futures. Even in Camden, welfare rolls had dropped by half as people faced the new law. But just as striking is the fact that no one can point to any changes in community life following the law's enactment. There are no new businesses to speak of. No revitalization.

The old system was easy to get into and hard to leave. The new system is hard to get into and easy to leave. The old system welcomed Cynthia "Cookie" Pulliam when she had her first baby at 18 in 1976. "What took you so long," was the greeting she received from county workers when she showed up at the welfare office with her two-week old infant. She immediately secured a cash grant of $235 a month, enrolled in Medicaid, and started collecting food stamps. She had been living with her mother in public housing, but her new baby provided the keys to her own unit.

It was certainly easy to sign up: All one needed to qualify was to have a baby, but not a husband or a job. It was also hard to get off welfare. At that time, getting a job and giving up the cash grant meant giving up other benefits as well. Unless recipients actually stuck with a long-term training program, saying good-bye to a cash grant meant bidding adieu to Medicaid as well. And for every $3 earned, a recipient's rent, set at 30 percent of income, increased by $1. People could certainly work their way off welfare, and many did, including Cookie who left in 1990 for a job as a recreation aid at the community center in her public housing complex. But the decision was made more difficult by the need to give up benefits in exchange for what was often a meager wage. The combined welfare package, in other words, was a better deal. The Cato Institute found that in 1995 the average welfare package beat an $8-an-hour job. In New Jersey, the package amounted to a $12.75 an hour. For many low-skilled women, it was a deal that couldn't be beat—and was very hard to refuse.

The 1996 law changed this, as Derica Lee, now a 22-year-old single mother living in Camden can tell you. The system hardly welcomed her when she tried to sign up in 2000. In order to get her cash grant of $322 a month, her caseworker handed her a stack of papers and told her to get 50 employers to verify that she had contacted them seeking a job. She did have a job at McDonalds at one point, but she quit. "I couldn't take that," Derica told me, "because they wanted me to wash some toilets."

However, now the system no longer cared. Derica was again told to look for work. I call this the "hassle factor," and it more than anything else is responsible for the decrease in the country's welfare rolls. The new law allows states to give people two years to find a job. But having experienced one failed long-term job training program after the other, states more often than not have opted to put people right to work finding jobs. This was the case in New Jersey, where all clients must look for work. For those under 18, the job is to finish high school or secure a general equivalency degree.

For clients over 18, the job is to get a job. Those who have worked in the last year go straight to knocking on prospective employers' doors. Counties offer short-term programs to ready people for work, but the goal is work, and the programs keep a person busy 35 hours a week. "It don't make no sense to do all of that," said Derica. "If I get all that done, why not just get a job? It ain't worth it."[8] The hassle factor is extremely important in that it addresses the Samaritan's dilemma by raising the costs of using welfare.

Rutgers University sociologist Ted Goertzel started studying the attitudes of welfare recipients in 1992. At that time, welfare was seen as a force of nature, a lifeline that would always exist no matter what. "I would try to raise questions about what would you like to do for a career, for work," Goertzel told me. "And it was like talking to kids in grade school. Work was something that was very much far off, unrealistic, maybe they'd like to work with children, be a physician. It was nothing practical, nothing happening in the short term." Time limits changed this outlook. "They realize that they are going to have to find jobs, that they have to find some way to support themselves, and that they can't rely on the welfare system as a permanent security blanket," reports Goertzel. "The idea has gotten across."[9]

Polls support Goertzel's findings. A study by Mathematica Policy Research found that 80 percent of New Jersey's welfare clients knew the time they could received cash grants was limited.[10] Six in 10 said the law affected their decision to work. Even ACORN, a group that never met a handout it didn't give a hand to and which opposes welfare reform, admits that the new program has focused people's minds on work.

But that is only half of it. The other incentive change is that the new system is easy to leave—at least the cash grant component. Recall that when Blondie or Cookie wanted to trade their cash grants for jobs, they lost their health insurance and had to pay more rent. Often it wasn't worth it. Under the new Work First New Jersey program, Derica doesn't have to give up her health care when she takes a job. Medicaid, childcare vouchers, food stamps, and in some cases even public housing rents have been separated from the cash voucher. She is even allowed to keep some of the cash grant, losing only

$0.50 for every dollar earned. In giving up the cash grant, all one gives up is $322 a month for one child or $424 for two. The average wage of former welfare recipients in New Jersey is $7.31, so they are almost always better off financially with a job, especially when you add in the $3,000 federal earned income tax credit someone making $7 an hour receives. A study in New Jersey found that the average monthly income of former welfare recipients was $1,600, compared to $800 for those who remain on the rolls. This isn't limited to New Jersey, however. "The clear consensus of all the studies is that folks who are working are doing better than folks who stay on welfare," says Douglas Besharov, who studies welfare reform at the American Enterprise Institute.[11]

Work First New Jersey and other state welfare reforms have sought to remove every excuse a person could have for not having a job. In the 1960s the structural view of poverty had become accepted. This held that everyone wanted to work—after all, that is what they told pollsters. Therefore, the only reason a person wasn't working was because of some external barrier—lack of proper training, lack of transportation, or the need for childcare.

Since the 1960s, the federal government has sponsored hundreds of job training programs. None were successful in reducing poverty or even getting significant numbers of people to work. The states, given the freedom under the new law, decided the best job training is a job, and pushed people to get one as soon as possible. They may provide a two-week crash course in interviewing and etiquette, and some offer support during the first few months of employment, but they no longer send people to college.

The same is true for transportation. Very few people work within walking distance of where they live. Gloucester County, New Jersey, a rural county, used to provide $6 a day to welfare recipients for transportation. "Who knows what they did with the money," said William Gordon, the deputy director of the county's welfare program. He assumes that clients considered it a $120-a-month cash bonus. Work First New Jersey allowed Mr. Gordon to be creative. He converted the transportation stipend into bus passes, which cost half as much, and then set up a jitney service to get people to bus lines.[12]

When the option wasn't an extra fat welfare check, people came up with ways to get to work on their own, "All of a sudden they'd say, 'I think my uncle gave me a car last week,'" reports Gordon.[13] For clients who maintain long-term employment and demonstrate a need, the county uses the funds to help them purchase a car and insurance. The county's welfare roles had dropped 65 percent as of 2000, down to 685 cases, many of which are child-only.

The mother of all work-avoidance excuses is the need for childcare. By definition, most women on AFDC had small children so on its face the excuse made sense. But it doesn't any longer. The new law provides billions in childcare subsidies. In some states, New Jersey and Maryland among them, everyone who needs childcare assistance gets a voucher. But even without vouchers, childcare has turned out to be more an obstacle in the minds of welfare advocates than in reality. People are resourceful, and many find informal mechanisms—grandmothers or neighbors—for caring for their children.

So is the current system a success? It depends on the standard against which it is measured. Caseloads are certainly down significantly. More people are heading to work everyday and supporting themselves, at least in part. This is certainly a good thing. Work changes people. It is good for a person's self esteem, and it is good for children to see their parents paying their own way in the world. It provides a context for accomplishments. "I wake up and hit the floor smiling every morning," says Deborah Keys, who had been on and off welfare since 1971. "Even when I have problems I smile."[14]

Decreasing welfare roles should not be confused with decreasing dependence on government. One goal of the legislation was to "end dependence of needy parents on government by promoting job preparation, work, and marriage."[15] Paradoxically, the reform might actually increase the number of people dependent on government for some of their basic needs. De-linking other benefits from the welfare grant makes them available to more people, not just those willing to sign up for the cash grant.

Welfare reform is not entirely conservative reform; it is a synthesis of conservative and liberal ideas. In exchange for putting people to work, Congress agreed, in effect, to spend more money per person. The system has shifted from being a support system for single women with children to being a work support system. It is similar to farm subsidies, where the cash that keeps people in business is added to what they earn from their own efforts.

The bill also sought to "reduce the incidence of out-of-wedlock pregnancies" and "encourage the formation of and maintenance of two-parent families."[16] It is too early to tell, but count me as skeptical about much of this. I think incentives do matter, and eliminating the economic penalties against marriage will have an effect. But in general, I doubt the government's ability to micromanage personal lives.

Camden remains a desperate city. With all the talk about the culture of poverty, and the welfare system's cash grant being at the center of it, I expected that the thousands of people returning to work would have had some effect on business formation, and the like. Not one person I talked to could cite one single way that the community had changed for the better after welfare reform.

Welfare Policy Tomorrow

The 1996 welfare reform bill is up for reauthorization in 2002—and there are roadblocks in its way. The economy is in recession, and those who still prefer the old system will try extremely hard to get more money and regulations.

Liberals make use of any and all opportunities to build the state—and they anticipate them well in advance. As people went to work, and it became clear that liberal doomsaying wasn't coming to pass, they changed their chant from "there are no jobs" to "what will happen in the next recession?" Now that we are smack in the middle of it, or—if Alan Greenspan is to be believed—on the way out, the liberals are talking about unemployment insurance. The Urban Institute came out with a study that shows that those former welfare recipients who have returned to work haven't worked long enough to qualify for state unemployment insurance programs.[17]

Nonetheless, this is progress. After all, to qualify for unemployment payments one must first have been employed.

The press has already begun to trumpet the liberal cause. Consider the bias in this lead in a *New York Times* article written by Robert Pear: "A year-long struggle over welfare policy will begin on Thursday and House Democrats offer a proposal to convert the 1996 welfare law into a tool for reducing poverty, while extending its provisions for five years."[18] Convert it into a tool to fight poverty? This recalls a bumper sticker from a less politically correct era: "Fight Poverty. Get a Job." By applying this slogan, the 1996 welfare law has proved to be the best tool yet for fighting poverty. According to the Census Bureau, child poverty had dropped from 20.5 percent to 16.2 percent since 1996.[19]

That is not what traditional welfare advocates have in mind. They want states to spend even more money—$150 million a year— to reduce child poverty, increase the general grant, and loosen the work requirements. And, of course, they want to bump the child-care block grant from $4.7 billion to $8 billion a year in 2007, a total increase of $11.25 billion.

Those who would like to return to the past have plenty of allies. Politicians at all levels of government have insatiable appetites for taxpayer money. The 1996 welfare reform law provided states with a windfall: The grants were frozen at record high levels even as welfare rolls emptied. The states spent the money on other programs and now, even though they are spending only 75 percent of 1996 expenditures (state funds), they have the gall to ask for more.

"When we took the block grant, we took the economic risk," Raymond C. Scheppach, the executive director of the National Governors Association, told the *New York Times*. "What we're saying now is that we are still willing to do that, except when there is a huge economic disruption."[20] In other words, even though they have been blessed with record levels of funding, they want more, more, more.

Since there has been no philosophical shift from the idea that the government ought to support people—if anything the group of those who ought to be supported has expanded—I think welfare reform's reauthorization will be a major backbone check for Congress, as well as for President Bush's compassionate conservatism. Can they handle success? Or will they use the increased generosity of the 1996 Welfare Reform law to launch yet another expansion of the welfare state?

Notes

[1] Charles Murray, *Losing Ground: American Social Policy 1950–1980* (New York: Basic Books, 1984), p. 46.

[2] Ibid., p. 29.

[3] Author's interview, March 2000. See Michael W. Lynch, "The Hassle Factor: Welfare Reform Turns Check Recipients into Job Seekers," *Reason Magazine* (December 2000): <http://reason.com/0012/ml.the.shtml>.

[4] Robert Rector, "The Size and Scope of Means-Tested Welfare Spending." Testimony before the United States House of Representatives, August 1, 2001, pp. 5–6.

[5] Ibid, p. xv.

[6] Lyndon B. Johnson, quoted in Murray, *Losing Ground*, p. 23

[7] Daniel Patrick Moynihan, quoted in Lynch, "The Hassle Factor."

[8] Author's interview, March 2000.

[9] Author's interview, March 2000.

[10] "How Work First New Jersey Clients are Faring under Welfare Reform: An Early Look," *Mathematica Policy Research* (October 21, 1999): 39.

[11] Author's interview, May 2000.

[12] Author's interview, March 2000.

[13] Author's interview, March 2000.

[14] Author's interview, March 2000.

[15] Public Law 104–193 Sec. 401(a)(2).

[16] Public Law 104–193 Sec. 401(a)(4).

[17] Harry J. Holzer, "Unemployment Insurance and the Recipient: What Happens When the Recession Comes?" *The Urban Institute* (December 2000): <http://www.urban.org>.

[18] Robert Pear, "House Democrats Propose Making the '96 Welfare Law an Antipoverty Weapon," *New York Times* (January 24, 2002): A24.

[19] Census Bureau, "Historical Poverty Tables: Table 3."

[20] Raymond Hernandez and Nina Bernstein, "Welfare Rolls Grew in City Late Last Year," *New York Times* (January 17, 2002): B1.

LAWRENCE M. STRATTON

Privilege Before the Law
is Trumping
Equality Before the Law

A tragic irony faces the world's most powerful nation as the third millennium begins. Almost four decades after the Civil Rights Act of 1964, and almost five decades after the landmark 1954 Supreme Court public school desegregation ruling of *Brown* v. *Board of Education*, the United States is developing into a premodern, feudal legal system in which legal standing is increasingly defined by race and gender status. A hardened regime is emerging in which the doors to employment, education, and promotion are not determined by character, as the Reverend Dr. Martin Luther King, Jr. envisioned in his famous 1963 speech in Washington, D.C., but by the color of a person's skin, and the shape of an individual's genitalia.

In the United States, equality under the law has given way to privilege in the law. Groups arbitrarily designated as "preferred minorities" by unaccountable federal bureaucrats and judges are routinely given access to universities, law schools, medical schools, employment, training programs, promotions, mortgage lending, and financial aid on easier terms than others, especially white males. The Congressional Research Service has identified over 160 federal programs alone that assign group privileges to "preferred minorities" and women.

Justice John Marshall Harlan's famous declarations that "there is no caste here. Our Constitution is color-blind" and "all citizens are equal before the law" are routinely derided by critical race theorists and so-called civil rights activists for entrenching white privilege with neutral rules. Race and gender quotas, balancing schemes, and preferences pervade the American legal and economic system. Whoever the beneficiary and however noble the motive, the casualty is equality before the law—the historic achievement that separates modern society with equal individual rights from feudalism with its array of disparate group rights. America begins the new millennium entrenched in the quicksand of status-based legal privileges of the premodern, preliberal era.

Equality before the law is a historic achievement that took a long time in coming. The principle freed people from the constraints of birth, privilege, and class. Alexis de Tocqueville captured the essence of this revolutionary change when he wrote more than 150 years ago that "aristocracy made a chain of all members of the community, from the peasant to the king; democracy breaks that chain and severs every link of it." Liberalism replaced the ancient regime "with a new social and political order, at once simple and more uniform, based on the concept of the equality of all men." Liberalism is summed up in a single word, "citizen," the enemy of class rank. In place of different courts with different laws for different classes of people—even legal restrictions on what clothes people of various ranks could wear and what food they could eat—the people of a country in the liberal order became united as citizens with equal standing under the law.

The disparate privileges of a status-based society are so long forgotten that it is useful to recall their injustice. Before the advent of the liberal precept of equality before the law, the legal requirement that judges weigh the distinctions of persons in dispensing justice made a person's status a threshold issue before the courts could address the merits of any legal claim. The status of the parties had to be determined first, because the set of legal burdens to which a person was then subjected depended on it. Status adjudication was also necessary because different courts had jurisdiction over different types of people. Freemen, for example, were permitted to file claims in the King's court, while villains were not.

In order to determine the class into which a person was born, courts sometimes even had to determine the place where conception occurred. Bracton, the twelfth-century English jurist, set down the rule to determine the status of a child born from the union of a freeman and a serf. Whether the child's legal status was that of a freeman or a villein depended upon "whether the child was the result of intercourse in the villein tenement or outside it, in a free bed."

In the feudal order, there were no First Amendment rights. Nobles were often protected against the verbal abuse of commoners by special provisions of the law. In places such as Lithuania, commoners who defamed nobles had their tongues cut out, something akin to Ivy League "free speech" codes. The English privilege of *scandalum magnatum* gave nobles special privileges to sue their critics for slander and free reign to verbally harass others. Nobles were also legally entitled to command silence and respect when they entered and departed public buildings.

Wergild laws specified fines not by crime, but by the status of the victim. After the Norman conquest in 1066, William the Conqueror expanded upon this principle by increasing penalties for native English criminal defendants whose victims were of Norman descent. Attacks on Normans were worse in the eyes of the law than attacks on Englishmen. As a result, defendants used elaborate pedigrees, known as "presentations of Englishry," to prove that their victims were English.

Such status-based legal distinctions were swept away by liberalism. For the first time in history, the liberal concept of individualism gave people an identity separate from their group status. According to the liberal ideal, rather than being a member of an estate, the vassal of a lord, or a slave, a person's legally relevant membership was as citizen of the nation, and all citizens were entitled to the same rights. Although the word citizen had been used in premodern monarchical societies to distinguish inhabitants of cities or towns from landed nobility or gentry, in the liberal era all members of the society became known as citizens.

Liberalism ushered in a meritocracy that displaced family rank as the critical factor in determining lifetime opportunities. In the nineteenth century Henry Sumner Maine, a law professor at Cambridge and Oxford, observed that "the movement of the progressive societies has hitherto been a movement from status to contract." Liberal societies had moved from "one terminus of history," in which all of a person's legal relationships flowed from his or her status, toward a new "social order in which all these relations arise from the free agreement of individuals."

In a meritocracy, individuals are free from feudal ties and can sell their services in the market. With the freedom to trade and move about, people could freely bargain and advance themselves based on their own thrift, industry, and good fortune. During the French Revolution, this liberal theme was summarized in the rallying cry "la carriere ouverte aux talents"—"a career open to the talents." Every man had the right to push to his full potential. In America, liberalism's pathway for merit was called the opportunity society. In 1793, lexicographer Noah Webster proclaimed that "the road is open for the poorest citizen to amass wealth by labor and economy, and by his talent and virtue to raise himself to the highest offices of the State."

By unleashing talent from the tethers of feudal privilege, equality before the law not only freed the individual, but strengthened society by increasing economic activity and creating wealth. In 1776 Adam Smith described in *The Wealth of Nations* how competitive forces were matching opportunity with merit. Smith drew upon the ideas of the French physiocrats, especially François Quesnay, author of the 1758 classic *Tableau economique*. The physiocrats helped set the French Revolution in motion by advocating an end to artificial impediments to the natural economic order, such as feudal dues, guild and manorial monopolies, and class privileges. According to Quesnay, France would become prosperous when all artificial restraints were removed.

Today the distinctive liberal historic achievements of equality before the law, and its corollary—respect for the democratic process in which "We the People" rule, rather than privileged elites—is endangered. The race, gender, handicapped, and increasingly sexual orientation status of Americans has become the controlling factor in court cases, in the workplace, and at college. Where liberal government was once based on a deep trust in the wisdom and goodwill of citizens and the subordination of government to the consent of the governed, the ruling premise of government and American ideological elites today is that race and gender interests have erected hegemonic discriminatory structures in law and employment that must be broken up by government coercion. Privilege before the law has displaced the ideal of equality before the law.

The civil rights movement wasn't supposed to end up this way. When Democratic Minnesota Senator Hubert Horatio Humphrey defended the 1964 Civil Rights Act during the Southern Democratic filibuster, he denied the charge that under the proposed statute, federal bureaucrats could force companies to establish hiring quotas. He said, "If the senator can find . . . any language which provides that an employer will have to hire on the basis of percentage or quota related to color, race, religion, or national origin, I will start eating the pages one after another, because it is not in there." For the past 37 years, bureaucrats, judges, and other government officials, both Republican and Democrat, have, in effect, been stuffing quotas down Senator Humphrey's throat.

Nobel prize-winning economist Gary Becker demonstrated in his classic 1957 book, *The Economics of Discrimination*, that markets don't discriminate because it doesn't pay. Becker showed that racial (and gender) discrimination is costly to those who practice it and thereby sets in motion forces that inexorably reduce it. Meritorious employees who are underpaid and underutilized because of their race will work elsewhere where they get paid according to their contributions to profit. An employer, for example, who hires a less qualified white because of prejudice against blacks will disadvantage herself in competition against those who hone their edge with the best employees that they can find. But this basic economic argument did not appeal to bureaucrats charged with enforcing the Civil Rights Act's prohibition on discrimination in employment.

In the last week of debate over the Civil Rights Act, in June 1964, Arizona Senator Barry Goldwater, who had just wrestled the Republican presidential nomination from New York Governor Nelson Rockefeller in the California primary, announced his opposition to the Civil Rights bill. Although Goldwater supported the provisions of the proposed statute that codified *Brown* v. *Board of Education* by ending discrimination by government, he feared that the bill commingled private and public life in a manner that permitted the tentacles of government regulation to enter the inner sanctum of individual conscience, especially in the bill's employment title, that he thought would take America across a watershed that "could ultimately destroy the freedom of all American citizens." Goldwater considered civil rights reform to be "fundamentally a matter of the heart," beyond the reach of government coercion.

Goldwater disagreed with his Republican colleague, Senate Minority Leader Everett Dirksen (R-IL), over whether the statute would lead to federally coerced racial quotas. Dirksen had broken the Senate filibuster, and earned the praise of Senator Humphrey, by inserting what is probably the longest sentence in the English language as an amendment to the act. Its 170 words, titled "Preferential treatment not to be granted on account of existing number or percentage imbalance," expressly and unambiguously forbade quotas.

Dirksen, presumably naively, thought that federal statutory language enacted by Congress binds federal bureaucrats and federal judges. Friedrich A. Hayek warned in *The Constitution of Liberty* that "the greatest danger to liberty today comes from the men who are most needed and most powerful in modern government, namely, the efficient expert administrator exclusively concerned with what they regard as the public good." These bureaucrats, Hayek said, inevitably skirt democratic control and make the administrative state "a self-willed and uncontrollable apparatus before which the individual is helpless."

The Civil Rights Act of 1964 undertook to put the billions upon billions of employer–employee decisions through a government filter, now located at 18th and L Streets in Washington, D.C.—the Equal Employment Opportunity Commission (EEOC). Such a massive intrusion into private life had not previously occurred in a free society. Issuing interpretative guidelines, which were themselves illegal under both the Civil Rights Act and the 1946 Administrative Procedure Act, the EEOC, under the leadership of enforcement chief Alfred W. Blumrosen of Rutgers Law School, redefined discrimination away from intentional acts to statistical racial disparities.

A history of the EEOC prepared for the Johnson Presidential Library admitted that this statistical redefinition was on a collision course with the text and legislative intent of the Civil Rights Act. Blumrosen's own writings brag about his "free and easy ways with statutory construction" that earned him the reputation within the EEOC as a "loophole" expert. Yet, the U.S. Supreme Court accepted the EEOC's rewrite of the Civil Rights Act in the 1971 case of *Griggs* v. *Duke Power*, in which employment tests having an unintended statistically "disparate impact" on minorities were declared to be discriminatory. This ruling also ignored Senator John Tower's (R-TX) amendment to the statute that explicitly protected professionally developed employment tests! In language all too familiar to people who monitor the interplay between federal bureaucrats and judges, Chief Justice Warren Burger said in his unanimous opinion, "The administrative interpretation of the act by the enforcing agency is entitled to great deference."

At about the same time, the Nixon Administration proposed its "Philadelphia Plan," which required federal contractors to hire minorities according to "goals and timetables" in order to attain racially proportionate workforces. Nixon wrote in his memoirs that his administration wanted to show blacks "that we do care." Although the phrase "federal contractor" conjures up images of workers in hard hats busy with construction projects or weapons systems, as Hillsdale and Grove City colleges found out in their own courageous, but costly, stands against the emerging quota regime in the 1970s, colleges and universities are also considered to be federal contractors, because they receive federal funds for research grants and financial aid to students. Following the Labor Department's lead, Nixon's Department of Health, Education, and Welfare soon required similar "goals and timetables" for faculty hiring—thereby launching the current pervasive quota system in the American academy.

The carrot of government contracts and the stick of disparate impact liability under *Griggs* v. *Duke Power* quickly established quota preferences across American society. For corporate managers, hiring by the numbers was the only protection against discrimination lawsuits and the loss of lucrative government contracts. Senator

Dirksen's prohibition of quotas in the Civil Rights Act remained in the books but meant nothing.

In 1979, the Supreme Court completely jettisoned Dirksen's amendment in the case of *United Steelworkers* v. *Weber.* Justice William Brennan's 5–2 majority opinion said that the meaning of the 1964 Civil Rights Act could not be found in its statutory language of prohibiting quotas, but its "spirit" of enhancing the plight of blacks in the economy. Justice William Rehnquist's dissent, joined by Chief Justice Warren Burger, called the majority opinion "Orwellian." Rehnquist said, "By a tour de force reminiscent not of jurists such as Hale, Holmes, and Hughes, but of escape artists such as Houdini, the Court eludes clear statutory language, uncontradicted legislative history, and uniform precedent in concluding that employers are, after all, permitted to consider race in making employment decisions."

When Justice Brennan declared that the Civil Rights Act's "spirit" of helping minorities trumped the anti-quota "letter" of statute, he cited the late nineteenth-century Supreme Court case of *Church of the Holy Trinity* v. *The United States* in which Justice David Brewer's unanimous opinion declared that a prominent New York City Episcopal Church could hire an English rector in defiance of a federal immigration statute. Justice Brewer argued that American law was premised upon Christianity, that America is a Christian nation, and that the spirit of Christianity that permeated American jurisprudence outweighed the letter of the immigration statute.

Regardless of whether or not Justice Brewer's contention about Christianity and law was then true, it is significant to recognize that Brewer expressed the thinking of American intellectual elites in the 1890s. He was the son of a prominent New England family that included Cyrus Field, who laid the trans-Atlantic cable; David Dudley Field, a leader of the New York Bar; and his uncle, another Supreme Court Justice, Stephen Field, a Lincoln appointee from California. Like Brewer in the late nineteenth-century, Justice Brennan's viewpoint reflected the attitudes of political and intellectual elites in the late twentieth century, who are the most tenacious defenders of the today's quota regime.

Critical race theorists—such as Harvard law professor Lani Guinier, whom former President Bill Clinton wanted to be his Assistant Attorney General for Civil Rights—argue that color blindness is "cultural genocide" for blacks and that the concept of merit implies "white male standards." Sidney Willhelm wrote in the *Michigan Law Review* that "the very idea of Equality, of treating Blacks and Whites alike, is racist because it fails to take account of over three hundred years of racist oppression. Equal opportunity is a myth because it ignores the tremendous advantages that Whites retain." Critical race theorists advocate expanded quotas and minority preferences and privileges everywhere as the solution and they demonize whites, and especially white males. Syracuse University Professor Laurence Thomas argues that "white males have committed more evil cumulatively than any other class of people in the world." He writes that "the Crusades, American slavery, and the two World Wars, including the Holocaust should clinch this point."

Smith College professor Stanley Rothman has noted that any negative or offensive characterizations of women and minorities are prohibited on campuses by rules against the "stereotyping" of any group except white males, who can be denounced with impunity as racist, sexist, villainous, and evil beyond belief. As George F. Will put it, "Only one group is ineligible for the privileged status of victim: there can be no limits on speech about white males." *Washington Post* columnist Richard Cohen has complained that as a white male writer, "I am being told to butt out, that since I am a member of the Oppressor Class, I may not comment."

In the face of this moral intimidation, efforts to rollback the quota regime have failed. President Ronald Reagan never fulfilled his campaign promise to pick up his pen and repeal the executive order mandating federal contracting quotas. The Supreme Court's efforts to scale back quotas, and especially the "disparate impact" definition of discrimination, in a series of cases in 1989 were rebuffed by the 1991 Civil Rights Act, signed by President George Herbert Walker Bush and incredulously claimed as not codifying quotas by White House Counsel C. Boyden Gray, a Federalist Society icon. In fall 2001, President George W. Bush's Solicitor General,

Theodore Olson, defended federal contracting quotas and preferences for minorities and women using arguments that were identical to the Clinton administration's position on quotas!

The consequences of the quota regime may be utter societal disaster. Justice John Paul Stevens noted in a 1980 case upholding federal minority construction set-asides (*Fullilove* v. *Klutznick*) that "If the national government is to make a serious effort to define racial classes by criteria that can be administered objectively, it must study the precedents such as the First Regulation to the Reich Citizenship Law of November 14, 1935." Justice Stevens' comparison of American quotas to Nazi Germany is not farfetched. Within months of attaining power in 1933, Adolf Hitler promulgated the "Law Against the Overcrowding of German Schools and Institutions of Higher Learning," which limited the percentage of Jewish students to "the proportion of non-Aryans within the Reich German population." Justice Anthony Kennedy and Hoover Institution scholar Thomas Sowell have similarly compared the American quota regime's allocation of racial privileges to South African apartheid.

We may hope that the American people will one day wake up and demand the end of quotas and preferences in favor of equality before the law. But it may be too late. In 1996, the people of California, the nation's most culturally diverse state, voted in favor of the "California Civil Rights Initiative," which echoed the 1964 Civil Rights Act in stating that "the state shall not discriminate against, or grant preferential treatment to, any individual or group on the basis of race, sex, color, ethnicity, or national origin in the operation of public employment, public education, or public contracting." But as the initiative's organizers have conceded, state quotas and preferences remain California's practice. Early efforts to scale back federal quotas by the Republican Congress in 1995 were equally lost in the legislative hopper.

Quotas have taken on a life of their own. Oliver Wendell Holmes wrote in his famous 1892 *Harvard Law Review* article, "The Path of the Law," that the deepest human instincts lay the "foundation of the acquisition of rights by lapse of time." Having been around for a generation, quotas are now protected by squatter's rights. The legal term for squatter's rights is "adverse possession." The doctrine says that the holders of property not legally theirs can nevertheless keep it if sufficient time lapses.

French historian Marc Bloch's classic study, *Feudal Society*, shows how the emergence of feudal privileges followed the fall of Rome, in that aristocratic European kings and lords obtained over time hereditary property rights on what were initially temporary privileges. Bloch says that "every act, especially if it was repeated three or four times, was likely to be transformed into a precedent—even if in the first instance it had been exceptional or even frankly unlawful." As Paul Craig Roberts and I detail in *The New Color Line: How Quotas and Privilege Destroy Democracy*, the parallels between the evolution of quotas and the emergence of feudalism are striking.

Considering the headway that the quota push for equality of result has made in undermining equality before the law, the pervasiveness of quotas and preferences, and the lack of understanding of their origins and implications, the fight to reclaim law from privilege has barely begun. Ultimately either quotas will go or democracy will, because legal privileges based on status are incompatible with democracy's requirement of equal standing before the law.

Bibliography

Abernathy, Charles F. "When Civil Rights Go Wrong: Agenda and Process in Civil Rights Reform." *Temple Political and Civil Rights Law Review* 2, no. 2 (Spring 1993): 177–208.

Abram, Morris B. "Affirmative Action: Fair Shakers and Social Engineers." *Harvard Law Review* 99, no. 6 (April 1986): 1312–326.

Abrams, Elliott. "The Quota Commission." *Commentary* (October 1972).

Adler, Jerry; Mark Starr; Farai Chideya; Lynda Wright; Pat Wingert; and Linda Haac. "Taking Offense: Is this the new enlightenment on campus or the new McCarthyism?" *Newsweek* (December 24, 1990).

Anderson, Martin. *Imposters in the Temple: American Intellectuals are Destroying Our Universities and Cheating our Students of Their Future*. New York: Simon & Schuster, 1992.

Baldwin, Frances Elizabeth. *Sumptuary Legislation and Personal Regulation in England*. Baltimore: Johns Hopkins Press, 1926.

Becker, Gary S. *The Economics of Discrimination*. Chicago: University of Chicago Press, 1957, 2d ed. 1971.

Belz, Herman. *Equality Transformed: A Quarter-Century of Affirmative Action.* New Brunswick, NJ: Transaction, 1991.

Bloch, Marc. *Feudal Society.* Chicago: University of Chicago Press, 1961.

Blumrosen, Alfred W. *Black Employment and the Law.* New Brunswick, NJ: Rutgers University Press, 1971.

_____. "Strangers in Paradise: *Griggs* v. *Duke Power Co.* and the Concept of Employment Discrimination." *Michigan Law Review* 71 (November 1971): 59–110.

Brodhead, Michael J. *David J. Brewer: The Life of a Supreme Court Justice, 1837–1910.* Carbondale: South Illinois University Press, 1994.

Byrne, Jeffrey S. "Affirmative Action for Lesbians and Gay Men: A Proposal for True Equality of Opportunity and Workforce Diversity." *Yale Law & Policy Review* 11, no. 1 (1993): 47–108.

Cantor, Norman F. *The Civilization of the Middle Ages.* New York: Harper-Collins, 1993.

Capers, I. Bennett. "Sex(ual Orientation) and Title VII." *Columbia Law Review* 91, no. 5 (June 1991): 1158–87.

Cazel, Fred A., Jr., Ed. *Feudalism and Liberty: Articles and Addresses of Sidney Painter.* Baltimore: Johns Hopkins Press, 1961.

Cohen, Richard. "A Whiter Shade of Male." *Washington Post Magazine* (August 12, 1990).

Congressional Research Service. "Memo to the Honorable Robert Dole: Compilation and Overview of Federal Laws and Regulations Establishing Affirmative Action Goals or Other Preference Based on Race, Gender, or Ethnicity." Washington, D.C.: Library of Congress, February 17, 1995.

Dawidowicz, Lucy S. *The War Against the Jews.* 2d ed. New York: Seth Press, 1986.

_____, Ed. *A Holocaust Reader.* New York: Behrman House, 1976.

Delgado, Richard, and Jean Stefancic. "Critical Race Theory: An Annotated Bibliography." *Virginia Law Review* 79, no. 2 (March 1971): 1109–316.

De Tocqueville, Alexis. *Democracy in America.* Richard D. Heffner, ed. New York: Signet, 2001.

_____. *The Old Regime and the French Revolution.* A. P. Kerr, ed. New York: Doubleday, 1955.

Eastland, Terry. "George Bush's Quota Bill: The Dismaying Impact of Griggs." *Policy Review* (Summer 1991).

Friedman, Milton. *Capitalism and Freedom.* Chicago: University of Chicago Press, 1962.

Glembocki, Vicki. "How to Get Your Kid into Penn." *Philadelphia Magazine* (October 2002).

Goldwater, Barry M., with Jack Casserly. *Goldwater.* New York: Doubleday, 1988.

Graham, Hugh Davis. *The Civil Rights Era: Origins and Development of National Policy 1960–1972.* New York: Oxford University Press, 1990.

Gray, C. Boyden. "Disparate Impact: History and Consequence." *Louisiana Law Review* 54, no. 6 (July 1994): 1487–505.

Guiner, Lani. "[E]racing Democracy: The Voting Rights Cases." *Harvard Law Review* 108, no. 1 (November 1994): 109–37.

──────────. "Keeping the Faith: Black Voters in the Post-Reagan Era." *Harvard Civil Rights–Civil Liberties Law Review* 24, no. 2 (Spring 1989): 393–435.

──────────. "No Two Seats: The Elusive Quest for Political Equality." *Virginia Law Review* 77, no. 8 (November 1991): 1413–514.

Hayek, Friedrich A. *The Constitution of Liberty*. Chicago: University of Chicago Press, 1960.

Holmes, Oliver Wendell. "The Path of the Law." *Harvard Law Review* 10, no. 8 (March 1897): 457–78

Hook, Sidney, "Meese's Major Failure." Letter to the Editor, *Policy Review* (Summer 1990).

Kens, Paul. *Justice Stephen Field: Shaping Liberty from the Gold Rush to the Gilded Age*. Lawrence, KS: University Press of Kansas, 1997.

King, Martin Luther, Jr. "I Have a Dream." In *A Testament of Hope: The Essential Writings and Speeches of Martin Luther King, Jr.* James M. Washington, ed. San Francisco: HarperCollins, 1986.

Kuczynski, Marguerite, and Meek, Ronald L., Eds. *Quesnay's Tableaueconomique*. New York: Macmillan, 1972.

Maine, Henry Sumner. *Ancient Law: Its Connection with the Early History of Society and its Relation to Modern Ideas*. 1861. Reprint. New York: Dorsett Press, 1986.

Mauro, Tony. "Olson Surprises Washington by Backing Affirmative Plan." *Fulton County Daily Report* (August 15, 2001).

McDowell, Gary L. "Affirmative Inaction: The Brock-Meese Standoff on Federal Racial Quotas." *Policy Review* (Spring 1989).

Nixon, Richard. *RN: The Memoirs of Richard Nixon*. 2 vols. New York: Warner Books, 1979.

Roberts, Paul Craig, and Lawrence M. Stratton. *The New Color Line: How Quotas and Privilege Destroy Democracy*. Washington, D.C.: Regnery, 1995, 1997.

Rothman, Stanley. "Professors in the Ascendant." *Academic Questions* 2, no. 4 (Fall 1989): 45–51.

Seabury, Paul. "HEW & the Universities." *Commentary* (February 1972).

Smith, Adam. *The Wealth of Nations*. Andrew Skinner, ed. New York: Penguin, 2000.

Southern, R. W. *The Making of the Middle Ages*. New Haven: Yale University Press, 1953.

Sowell, Thomas. *Preferential Policies: An International Perspective*. New York: William Morrow, 1990.

──────────. "The New Racism on Campus." *Fortune* (February 13, 1989).

Sykes, Charles J. *The Hollow Men: Politics and Corruption in Higher Education*. Washington, D.C.: Regnery Gateway, 1990.

Thomas, Laurence. "Next Life, I'll Be White." *New York Times* (August 13, 1990): A15.

U.S. Department of Justice. Office of Legal Policy Report to the Attorney General, *Redefining Discrimination: Disparate Impact and the Institutionalization of Affirmative Action.* Washington, D.C., 1987.

U.S. Equal Employment Opportunity Commission Archives, Washington, D.C. "The Equal Employment Opportunity Commission During the Administration of President Lyndon B. Johnson: November 1963–January 1969." November 1, 1968.

Walsh, Edward. "Bush Backs Minority Program; High Court Brief Defends DOT Contracting Plan." *Washington Post* (August 11, 2001): A1.

Will, George F. "Liberal Censorship." *Washington Post* (5 November 1989): C7.

Willney, Sidney. "'The Supreme Court: A Citadel for White Supremacy.' Review of *Race, Racism and American Law,* by Derrick A. Bel, Jr." *Michigan Law Review* 79, no. 4 (March 1981): 847–55.

Wood, Gordon S. *The Radicalism of the American Revolution.* New York: Alfred A. Knopf, 1992.

Congressional Record

Goldwater, Sen. Barry. *Congressional Record,* 110, pt. 11 (18 June 1964): 14319.

Humphrey, Sen. Hubert H. *Congressional Record,* 110, pt. 4 (17 March 1964): 5423.

Humphrey, Sen. Hubert H. *Congressional Record,* 110, pt. 5 (30 March 1964): 6549, 6552–553.

Humphrey, Sen. Hubert H. *Congressional Record,* 110, pt. 6 (9 April 1964): 7420.

Humphrey, Sen. Hubert H. *Congressional Record,* 110, p. 10 (4 June 1964): 12707, 12722–2724.

Humphrey, Sen. Hubert H. *Congressional Record,* 110, pt. 10 (13 June 1964): 13724.

Court Cases

Adarand Constructors, Inc. v. *Pena,* 515 U.S. 200 (1995).

Adarand Constructors, Inc. v. *Mineta,* 534 U.S. 103 (2001).

Brown v. *Board of Education* v. *Topeka,* 347 U.S. 483 (1954).

Church of the Holy Trinity v. *United States,* 143 U.S. 457 (1892).

Contractors Association of Eastern Pennsylvania v. *Secretary of Labor,* 442f.2d 159 (3rd Cir. 1971), cert. Denied, 404 U.S. 854 (1971).

Fullilove v. *Klutznick,* 448 U.S. 448 (1980).

Griggs v. *Duke Power Co.* 401 U.S. 424 (1971).

Johnson v. *Transportation Agency,* Santa Clara County, Calif., 480 U.S. 616 (1987).

Metro Broadcasting, Inc. v *FCC,* 497 U.S. 547 (1990).

Plessy v. *Ferguson,* 163 U.S. 537 (1896).

Regents of the University of California v. *Bakke,* 438 U.S. 265 (1978).

Richmond v. *J. A. Croson, Co.,* 488 U.S. 469 (1989).

United Steelworkers of America v. *Weber,* 443 U.S. 193 (1979).

Wards Cove Packing Co. v. *Atonio,* 490 U.S. 642 (1989).

Mark R. Levin

The Americans with Disabilities Act: A Model of Bureaucratic Regulation

The Americans with Disabilities Act (ADA) has the potential for being the mother of all bureaucratic idiocy.

The ADA became law on July 26, 1990. Two of the major proponents of the bill were then-President George Bush and Senator Bob Dole, which indicates that Republicans are not always the principled opponents of big government. In addition to spearheading the passage of the ADA, the Environmental Protection Agency and the Occupational Safety and Health Administration became law thanks to Republican support.

The true nature and consequences of these laws are usually masked with wonderful sounding titles. Take the Endangered Species Act. It would be more accurate to call it the Job Killing Act or the Property Stealing Act. The Environmental Protection Agency would more accurately be described as the Department of Junk Science or the Safe House for Environmental Wackos.

Demanding accountability from these agencies, or requiring them to live within a reasonable budget, or attempting to modify the various laws that have been so distorted through bureaucratic regulation, lawsuits, and judicial decrees, could position a person to be accused of opposing the environment, or opposing worker safety, or, in the case of the ADA, opposing the plight of the disabled. To many people, the federal bureaucracy and federal law have come to stand for the entire universe of God-given liberties and rights.

From the middle of 1992 through fiscal year 2000, approximately 150,000 charges have been filed under the ADA, including those filed concurrently under other statutes. The charges are made first to the Equal Employment Opportunity Commission (EEOC), after which a private claim can be brought in federal court. If an administrative resolution is not possible and the agency feels strongly enough about a particular matter, a claim can be brought by the EEOC.

The EEOC reports that since the inception of the ADA nearly 53 percent of the charges filed with that agency have been found to have no reasonable cause—that is, there is no reasonable basis to believe there was discrimination. Although I was unable to find statistics that reveal the number of these cases that wind up in federal court, the potential for a litigation explosion exists in the law itself.

The ADA covers "disabled" individuals. This includes people with physical or mental impairments that substantially limit one or more of their major life activities; people who have a record of such an impairment; and people who are regarded as having such an impairment. If this sounds lucid to you, then maybe you qualify for benefits under one of these tests.

Others protected under the act include people associated with individuals who have disabilities, such as a guardian or parent, and people who are coerced or retaliated against for helping the disabled assert their rights under the ADA.

The act's employment provisions cover businesses with 15 or more employees. The public accommodation provisions apply to all businesses, and local and state governments, of any size.

I used to think that when Congress passes laws such as the ADA, it is motivated by good intentions that, nonetheless, create unintended consequences. I don't think that anymore. We have had enough experience with the outrages and excesses of big government by now to know that the bureaucracies, the trial lawyers, and the courts have never read a statute they couldn't distort and expand. The ADA is no exception.

A federal lawsuit titled *EEOC* v. *Exxon Corporation* was brought under the ADA. As Thomas Hungar wrote in *The Wall Street Journal* in 1999:

Exxon was subjected to billions of dollars in cleanup costs, monetary claims, punitive damage awards and criminal sanctions for allegedly placing a recovering alcoholic in command of a supertanker. It took the lesson to heart and decided to prohibit employees with a history of alcohol and drug abuse from holding safety-sensitive positions. The same U.S. government that exacted a huge fine for the "crime" of placing Captain Joseph Hazelwood in charge of the Exxon *Valdez* is now suing Exxon, claiming that the ADA requires the company to permit future Hazelwoods to assume similar positions.[1]

A settlement the Justice Department negotiated with Exxon included the adoption of a safety policy in relation to the employment of former alcoholics and drug addicts. That is the policy that EEOC challenged.

Most of us would consider Exxon's position of prohibiting employees with a history of substance abuse from holding safety-sensitive positions reasonable and responsible. But the EEOC did not. It claimed that Exxon's policy violated the agency's "interpretive guidance" requiring Exxon to demonstrate that each individual could not pose a "direct threat" to the health or safety of others in the workplace. In other words, the burden would be Exxon's to prove that a employee or job candidate poses a "direct threat" in the particular job. Exxon answered that it cannot be sure that a recovering alcoholic or drug addict won't relapse, and it cannot police every situation.

Although the Fifth Circuit Court rejected the EEOC's position, its conclusions could have been a lot clearer. For instance, in considering whether an across-the-board policy is justified, the court said that there are certain factors that need to be considered, such as the magnitude of the possible harm and the probability of occurrence. How are you supposed to determine this? The court said: "A probability that might be tolerable in an ordinary job might be intolerable for a position involving atomic reactors."[2]

Exxon entered into a settlement with one part of the federal government, the Justice Department, and was sued over that settlement by another part of the federal government, the EEOC. A federal appellate court upheld Exxon's safety policy, but then created an ambiguous standard for the application of such a safety policy. And they say the law is an ass! This is what passes as legal guidance for employers? The law should be clear enough to provide employers with notice of their responsibilities. It shouldn't set them up for future litigation.

The Supreme Court recently made a determination regarding the ADA in *Toyota Motor Manufacturing* v. *Williams.* Ella Williams, an assembly line worker at a Toyota manufacturing plant, claimed to have become disabled from performing her job, and so she sued Toyota for failing to provide reasonable accommodations under the ADA. Williams claimed that due to carpal tunnel syndrome, she was unable to hold her hands and arms at shoulder height for several hours at a time. The issue in litigation was whether such an impairment constituted a disability under the ADA.

The District Court held that Williams' impairment did not qualify as a disability "because it had not substantially limited any major life activity and that there was no evidence that [Williams] had a record of a substantially limiting impairment."[3] The Court of Appeals found that William's impairment did substantially limit the major life activity of performing manual tasks.

The Supreme Court reversed the Court of Appeals, holding that the "Sixth Circuit did not apply the proper standard in determining that [Williams] was disabled because it analyzed only a limited class of manual tasks and failed to ask whether [Williams'] impairments prevented or restricted her from performing tasks that are of central importance to most people's daily lives."[4]

In determining whether a person is disabled under the ADA, the "central inquiry must be whether the claimant is unable to perform the variety of tasks central to most people's daily lives."[5] Such activities include household chores, bathing, and brushing one's teeth.

Last year, the Supreme Court issued a number of ADA decisions, including *Sutton* v. *United Airlines,* in which it held that the ADA did not apply to nearsighted twin sisters who applied to United for jobs as airline pilots. The reason: Eyeglasses corrected their vision problems.[6]

In *Murphy* v. *United Parcel Service*, the Court held UPS had not discriminated against a mechanic who was dismissed because he had very high blood pressure because his condition was treatable.[7] In *Albertsons, Inc.* v. *Kirkingburg*, the High Court said the supermarket chain did not violate the ADA when it fired a truck driver who was nearly blind in one eye.[8] In *Olmstead* v. *L.C.*, the Court ruled that the ADA requires states to move people with certain mental problems from mental hospitals to community homes.[9]

In an article for the Cato Institute last year, Julie Hofius, an attorney who uses a wheelchair, wrote that she can now get through most doorways and proceed down most hallways.[10] She said that while she can overcome most physical obstacles, employers are now less likely to hire the disabled because of fear of lawsuits. A Harris survey for the National Organization on Disability conducted in 2002 found that only 29 percent of disabled people were employed full- or part-time, down from 33 percent in 1986.[11] Hofius logically concludes that employers haven't become more prejudiced. They have become more concerned that the vague language of the ADA will invite more lawsuits.

Last year, the Supreme Court also ruled in the much-reported Casey Martin/PGA Tour case. Martin has a rare leg ailment that makes it very difficult for him to walk. The PGA prohibits its members from using golfcarts, which eliminated Martin from PGA play.

By a 7–2 vote, the Supreme Court ruled for Casey. Justice John Paul Stevens, writing for the majority, concluded that tournament golf was a "public accommodation" and that Martin's use of a cart would not "fundamentally alter the nature" of the game.[12]

The PGA argued that the "public accommodation" requirement applied to spectators, not professional golfers. Stevens decreed that it applied to golfers since golfers are the actual customers of golf. Stevens also ruled that walking is not an important part of golf, shot-making is. He wrote that "pure chance may have a greater impact on the outcome of elite golf tournaments than the . . . enforcement of the walking rule."[13]

The dissent was written by Antonin Scalia, joined by Clarence Thomas. Scalia pointed out that "professional ballplayers participate in the games, and use the ball fields, but no one in his right mind would think that they are customers of the American League or Yankee Stadium." Scalia wrote further that the rules "are entirely arbitrary, and there is no basis on which anyone—not even the Supreme Court of the United States—can pronounce one or another of them to be 'nonessential' if the rule maker deems it essential.'" Scalia added that "the Court should decline to answer this incredibly difficult and incredibly silly question."[14]

So now we have the courts running professional sporting games. The Supreme Court has given a host of athletes hope. *The Wall Street Journal* reported recently that "New England Patriot wide receiver Terry Glenn, in a suit filed this week against the NFL, claims he's covered by the ADA. Mr. Glenn says he's depressed and therefore, under the ADA, shouldn't have been subject to a four-game suspension earlier in the season for failing to comply with a substance abuse policy. The suspension triggered a clause in his contract that cost him $8.75 million on his signing bonus. Mr. Glenn is not on the roster to play in Sunday's Super Bowl; the touchdown he's hoping for is in the ADA case."[15]

Why was the Americans with Disabilities Act passed? Was there widespread evidence of discrimination against the disabled in hiring and firing practices? Was there widespread evidence of discrimination in public accommodations?

The assumption in the passage of the ADA, as in other federal laws of this kind, is that only the federal government—not the American people—can be trusted to do the right thing. That unlike the private sector—which is out to punish the disabled, the elderly, single mothers, minorities, and others—the federal government is righteous in all respects. The notion is that when a private citizen ascends to federal office, whether elected or employed as part of the vast federal bureaucracy, that person is suddenly transformed from an ignorant grunt into an expert who is wise in all matters. Have you ever wondered how Ted Kennedy, who has spent virtually his entire working career in the Senate, can know so much about all matters? Joe Biden was 29 when he was elected to the Senate. (He turned 30, the constitutionally required minimum age, before he was sworn in.) Despite his lack of experience, Biden served for many years as chairman of the Judiciary Committee. As chairman, he had enormous influence over our antitrust laws, our counterterrorism activities, and a slew of other areas in which he had no substantial knowledge.

But this is representative government, you say. Our senators and congressmen need not be experts. They need only persuade enough people to vote for them to achieve high office. But this misses the point. The Declaration of Independence celebrates the nature of man, the God-given enlightenment we all have, which is the foundation of a free society. The constitution creates a limited central government. The powers are enumerated and divided—both within the central government itself and as between the central government and the state governments. The framers had a very different view of private citizens and the private sector than do most Democrats and many Republicans today. They didn't believe the central government would be dispensing rights and privileges without any real limitation. They saw man as good, not as the subject of conquest.

Though impossible to accurately assess, the economic impact of laws like the ADA is very significant. Even though over half of the charges brought to the EEOC have been dismissed, the most absurd charges continue to be brought into federal court. The cost of this litigation is enormous, both in terms of direct expenditures and lost time and opportunity costs.

The ADA discourages voluntary remediation. In fact, it doesn't even require consultation before filing a complaint. The behavior that is rewarded is confrontational and litigious. There are members of Congress who are trying to amend the law, but they have been unsuccessful because a powerful special interest lobby is opposed to any changes.

By federalizing procedures, definitions, and standards, local governments are taken out of the equation. Local governments are traditionally more responsive to the needs of the people who live in their neighborhoods. Distant bureaucrats don't have a stake in the local community—and they often have a very different agenda.

The ADA is law, but a liberal's job is never done. So it is on to bigger things, like passing a national prescription drug entitlement and a so-called Patients' Bill of Rights. The people simply can't be trusted to do the right thing.

Notes

[1]Thomas G. Hungar, "Clear-Sighted View of the ADA," *The Wall Street Journal* (24 June 1999): A22.

[2] *EEOC* v. *Exxon Corp.*, 203 F.3d 871 (5th Cir. 2000)

[3]*Toyota Motor Manufacturing* v. *Williams*, 534 U.S. 184, 151 L.Ed. 2d 615, 122 S.Ct 681 (2002).

[4]Id. @ 687.

[5]Id. @ 687.

[6]*Sutton* v. *United Airlines, Inc.*, 527 U.S. 471 (1999).

[7]*Murphy* v. *United Parcel Service*, 527 U.S. 516 (1999).

[8]*Albertsons, Inc.* v. *Kirkingburg*, 527 U.S. 555 (1999).

[9]*Olmstead* v. *L.C.*, 527 U.S. 581 (1999).

[10]Julie Hofius, "How the ADA Handicaps Me," July 26, 2000, <www.cato.org/dailys/07-26-000.html>.

[11]Ibid.

[12]*P.G.A. Tour, Inc.* v. *Martin*, 532 U.S. 661, 149 L.Ed. 2d 904, 121 S.Ct. 1879 (2001).

[13]Id. @ 1893.

[14]Id. @ 1904.

[15]"ADA Super Bowl,"*The Wall Street Journal* (February 1, 2002): A18.

SALLIE BALIUNAS

The Kyoto Protocol and Global Warming

The evolution from fire to fossil fuels to nuclear energy is a path of improved human health and welfare arising from efficient and effective access to energy. One trade-off is that energy use by human beings has always produced environmental change. For example, it has resulted in human artifacts marking the landscape, the removal of trees from major areas for wood burning, and regionwide noxious air pollution from coal burning. On the other hand, ready availability of energy that produces wealth through the free market system provides ways to remedy or minimize environmental damage from energy use.

With widespread industrialization, human use of coal, oil, and natural gas has become the centerpiece in an international debate over a global environmental impact, viz., global warming. Fossil fuels provide roughly 84 percent of the energy consumed in the United States and 80 percent of the energy produced worldwide. An attempt to address the risk of deleterious global warming from the use of these carbon dioxide-emitting fuels is embodied in the Kyoto Protocol and its attendant series of international negotiations. But on scientific, economic, and political grounds, the Kyoto Protocol as an attempt to control this risk while improving the human condition is flawed.

Views express here do not necessarily reflect those of any institution with which the author is affiliated.

What Would Kyoto Do?

Projections of future energy use, applied to the most advanced computer simulations of climate, have yielded wide-ranging forecasts of future warming from a continued increase of carbon dioxide concentration in the air. The middle-range forecast of the estimates of the United Nations Intergovernmental Panel on Climate Change, based on expected growth in fossil fuel use without any curbs, consists of a one degree Celsius increase over the next half century. A climate simulation including the effect of implementing the Kyoto Protocol—negotiated in 1997 and calling for a worldwide 5 percent cut in carbon dioxide emissions from 1990 levels—would reduce that increase to approximately 0.94 degree Celsius. This amounts to an insignificant 0.06 degree Celsius averted temperature increase. (See Chart 1. The jagged line tracks the forecast of increasing temperatures through 2050, based on the Hadley Center's model. The upper straight line is the linear trend fit to the model's forecast temperature rise without implementation of Kyoto, and the lower straight line is the linear trend with implementation.)

To achieve the carbon dioxide emission cuts by 2012 that are required under the Kyoto agreement, the United States would have to slash its projected 2012 energy use by about 25 percent. Why, then,

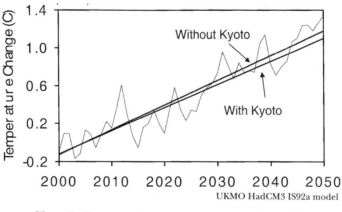

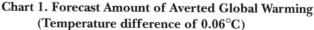

**Chart 1. Forecast Amount of Averted Global Warming
(Temperature difference of 0.06°C)**

are the temperature forecasts so minimal in terms of averted global warming? The answer is that countries like China, India, and Mexico are exempt from making emission cuts, and China alone will become the world's leading emitter of carbon dioxide in just a few years.

Most economic studies indicate that the cost of the Kyoto carbon dioxide emission cuts to the U.S. would amount to between $100 billion and $400 billion per year. One major reason these costs are so high is that past U.S. energy policy has been constrained by political influences. For example, substantially expanding the number of U.S. nuclear power plants and reducing the number of coal plants would enable the U.S. to meet both its future energy needs and Kyoto's mandated carbon dioxide emission reductions. But no nuclear power plants have been built in the U.S. in over 20 years, owing to nontechnical factors.

Over the same period, renewable energy sources like wind and solar power have been discussed to the point of distraction. But these are boutique energy sources: They produce relatively minute amounts of energy and do so intermittently. While they may be cost-effective in limited locales, they are unreliable for large-scale electricity generation. (As a side note, often overlooked is the enormous environmental footprint that wind and solar farms would require. For example, to replace a conventional 1,000 megawatt coal plant that spans tens of acres would require an isolated, uninhabited area with correct meteorological conditions of roughly 400 square miles on which to place over 2,000 wind turbines, not to mention the associated imprint of high-power transmission lines, roads, etc. Solar panel farms would produce environmental blight and degradation over a similarly sized landscape.)

The Kyoto Protocol also has the potential to worsen international relations. The struggling economies of the world rely on the U.S. to maintain stability and to provide aid and economic opportunity as a trading partner. While the developing nations are exempt from making carbon dioxide emission cuts, the severe economic impact on the U.S. would dramatically curtail its ability to continue to promote international stability and to help improve those nations' economies.

What Does Science Say?

Whereas the economic catastrophe that would occur as a result of implementing the Kyoto Protocol is a certainty, the likelihood of an environmental catastrophe resulting from a failure to implement Kyoto is extremely speculative. The facts in scientific agreement concerning global warming are as follows:

- As a result of the use of coal, oil, and natural gas, the air's carbon dioxide content (along with the content of other human-produced greenhouse gases like methane) is increasing.
- The greenhouse gases absorb infrared radiation and, as a result, should retain some energy near the surface of the earth that would otherwise escape to space.
- Based on current ideas about how climate should work, the surface temperature should warm in response to the addition of the small amount of energy arising from a benchmark doubling of the air's carbon dioxide content.
- The main greenhouse effect is natural and is caused by water vapor and clouds. But the impacts of these greenhouse factors are for now greatly uncertain. In other words, the reliability of even the most sophisticated computer simulations of the climate impacts of increased carbon dioxide concentration rests heavily on the use of factors that science does not understand. To put this in perspective, the uncertainties surrounding the use of clouds and water vapor in climate simulations—not to mention other important factors like sea-ice changes—are at least ten times greater than the effect of the variable being tracked, that is, the temperature rise caused by increased carbon dioxide levels in the air.
- Finally, in the absence of any counterpoising or magnifying responses in the climate system, the global average rise in temperature is roughly one degree Celsius or less at equilibrium for a doubling of the air's carbon dioxide concen-

tration. That is meager warming for so profound a change in the air's carbon dioxide content. Indeed, it is within the range of climate's natural variability.

One key question in the debate over global warming is, What has been the response of the climate thus far to the small amount of energy added by humans from increased carbon dioxide in the air? This question is important because in order to prove the reliability of future climate forecasts from computer simulations those simulations need to prove that they are reliable at explaining past temperature change. They have not yet done so.

In the twentieth century, the global average surface temperature rose about 0.5 degrees Celsius. At first glance, one might think this attributable to human fossil fuel use, which has increased sharply over the past 100 years. But a closer look at twentieth-century temperatures shows three distinct trends. First, a strong warming trend of about 0.5 degrees Celsius began in the late nineteenth century and peaked around 1940. Then, oddly, there was a cooling trend from 1940 until the late 1970s. A modest warming trend occurred from the late 1970s to the present. (See Chart 2, illustrating surface temperature changes sampled worldwide and analyzed by Cambridge Research Unit [solid line] and NASA-Goddard Institute of Space Studies [dotted line]. Both lines show these three distinct phases in the twentieth century.)

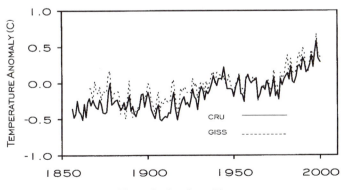

Chart 2. Surface Temperature

How do we interpret these data? We know that about 80 percent of the carbon dioxide from human activities was added to the air after 1940. Thus increased carbon dioxide in the air cannot account for the pre-1940 warming trend. That trend had to be largely natural. Then, as the air's carbon dioxide content increased most rapidly, temperatures dropped for nearly 40 years. And it seems that human effects amount at most to about 0.1 degree Celsius per decade—the maximum increase in warming seen after the 1970s.

How, then, does the observed surface-warming trend in recent decades—even assuming it is all due to human activity—compare to the results of climate change computer simulations?

Looking back at Chart 1, we note that climate simulations predict that a smooth linear rise of at least twice the observed trend should already be occurring, and that it will continue through the next century. Given that the warming trend has been observed to be at most 0.1 degree Celsius per decade from human activities, these future forecasts appear to greatly exaggerate the future warming and should be adjusted downward to, at most, one degree Celsius warming by 2100. That amount of warming would be similar to natural variability, which humans have dealt with for thousands of years. Indeed, it would likely return climate conditions to those experienced in the early centuries of the second millennium, when widespread warming was indicated by numerous proxies of climate, such as glaciers, pollen deposits, boreholes, ice cores, coral, tree growth, and sea and lake floor sediments. (It is interesting to note that this so-called Medieval Climate Optimum is associated with the settling of Greenland and Iceland, travel by the Vikings to Newfoundland, higher crop yields, and generally rising lifespans.)

New Data

In addition to what we can deduce from surface temperature data, U.S. leadership in developing new space instruments and in the funding of global research has yielded atmospheric temperature data that also indicate a lesser humanmade global warming trend than is forecast by climate simulations.

According to these simulations, a readily detectable warming of the lower troposphere (roughly 5,000 to 28,000 feet altitude) must occur with the presence of increased atmospheric carbon dioxide concentration. But records from NASA's microwave sounder units aboard satellites show no such trend. These satellite records are essentially global, in contrast with records of surface temperatures, which cover a mere one-fifth of the planet. What emerges from them is that while the tropospheric temperature does vary over short periods—for example, with the strong El Nino warming pulse of 1997 and 1998—no meaningful warming trend is observed over the 21-year span of the record. (See Chart 3, illustrating monthly averaged temperatures for the lower troposophere from instruments onboard NASA satellites. Even taking into account the 1997–1998 El Nino event, the linear trend is only +0.04 degree Celsius per decade. Data are from <www.ghcc.msfc.nasa.gov/temperature/>.)

It should be noted in passing that there has been a proposed explanation for the lack of a significant humanmade warming trend in the lower troposphere. This explanation contends that human-induced global warming is masked because of soot from sulfur dioxide and other humanmade aerosols, which cool the atmosphere. But this idea of a widespread aerosol shading effect fails the test by the scientific method, because the Southern Hemi-

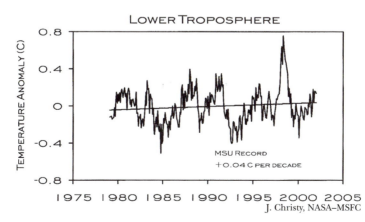

Chart 3. Global Temperature

sphere—which shows no long-term warming trend at all—is relatively free of aerosols.

In addition to satellite records, we have a radiosonde record from balloons that goes back over four decades. This record obviously lacks the dense spatial coverage of satellite measurements. Nevertheless, it too shows no warming trend in global average temperature that can be attributed to human effects. It records the strong warming in 1976–1977 known as the Great Pacific Climate Shift, resulting from a natural periodic shift in the Pacific—the Pacific Decadal Oscillation—which is so significant that global average temperatures are affected. (See Chart 4, which illustrates the seasonal average temperature anomaly sampled worldwide for the lower troposphere as measured by radiosonde instruments carried aboard balloons. Although a linear trend of +0.09 degree Celsius per decade is present if fitted across the entire period of the record, the trends before and after the abrupt warming of 1976–1977 [straight horizontal lines] indicate no evidence of significant humanmade warming. Data are from <cdiac.esd.ornl.gov/ftp/trends/temp/angell/glob.dat>.) Furthermore, the Pacific now seems to have shifted, perhaps in 1998–1999, back to its pre-1976 phase, which should produce cooler temperatures, especially in Alaska and in the global average.

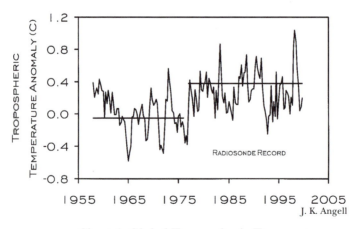

Chart 4. Global Tropospheric Temperature

Thus according to our most reliable data, when compared to the actual measurements of temperature over the past four decades, computer simulations overestimate to some degree the warming at the surface and decidedly exaggerate warming in the lower troposphere. And given that the models have overestimated past warming trends, they presumably also exaggerate the warming to be expected in the future. This inaccuracy is not surprising. Computer simulations of climate must track over five million parameters relevant to the climate system. To simulate climate change for a period of several decades is a computational task that requires 10,000,000,000,000,000,000 degrees of freedom. And to repeat, such simulations require accurate information on two major natural greenhouse gas factors—water vapor and clouds—whose effects we do not yet understand.

Finally, it should be mentioned that in looking for natural factors influencing the climate, a new area of research centers on the effects of the sun. The sun's magnetism varies in step with its total energy output. Measurements of the sun's total energy output are recent byproducts of the satellite era, but records of the sun's magnetism extend back nearly four centuries. Periods of high or low solar magnetism, lasting several decades or so, tend to correspond to warmer or cooler periods on the earth. (See Chart 5, illustrating the change over four centuries of the Sunspot Number, which is representative of the surface area coverage of the sun by strong magnetic fields. The low magnetism of the seventeenth century, a period called the Maunder Minimum, coincides with the coldest century of the last millennium, and there is sustained high magnetism in the latter twentieth century.) Twentieth-century temperature changes show a strong correlation with the sun's changing energy output. Although the causes of the sun's changing particle, magnetic, and energy outputs are uncertain—as are the responses of the climate to solar changes—the correlation is pronounced. It explains especially well the early twentieth-century temperature increase, which, as we have seen, could not have had much human contribution. (See Chart 6, showing that changes in the sun's magnetism—as evidenced by the changing length of the 22-year or Hale

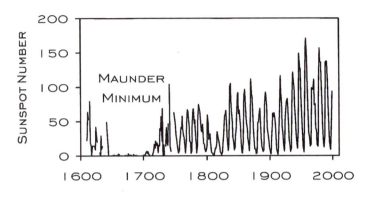

Chart 5. Sunspot Numbers, 1600 to 2000

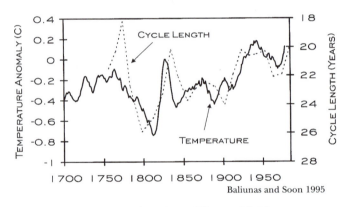

Baliunas and Soon 1995

Chart 6. A Sun–Climate Link?
Northern Hemisphere Land Temperature and Solar cycle

Polarity Cycle [dotted line]—closely correlates with changes in
Northern Hemisphere land temperature [solid line]. The sun's
shorter magnetic cycles are more intense, suggesting a brighter
sun during longer cycles. Lags or leads between the two curves
that are shorter than 20 years are not significant, owing to the 22-
year timeframe of the proxy of brightness change. In this chart,
the record of reconstructed Northern Hemisphere land temperature substitutes for global temperature, which is unavailable back
to 1700.)

Conclusions

Two conclusions can be drawn about global warming and human energy use:

- No catastrophic humanmade global warming effects can be found in the best measurements of climate that we presently have.
- The longevity, health, welfare, and productivity of humans have improved with the use of fossil fuels for energy, and the resulting human wealth has helped produce environmental improvements beneficial to health as well.

In light of some of the hysterical language surrounding the issue of greenhouse gases, it is also worth noting that carbon dioxide, the primary greenhouse gas produced by burning fossil fuels, is not a toxic pollutant. To the contrary, it is essential to life on earth. And plants have flourished—agricultural experts estimate a 10 percent increase in crop growth in recent decades—due directly to the fertilization effect of increased carbon dioxide in the air.

It is good news, not bad, that the best current science offers little justification for the rapid cuts in carbon dioxide mandated by the Kyoto Protocol. This science indicates that humanmade global warming is relatively minor and will be slow to develop, affording us an opportunity to continue to improve observations and computer simulations of climate. These will serve to better define the magnitude of humanmade warming, and allow development of an effective and cost-effective response.

Given this science, what is impelling the Kyoto Protocol's international momentum? One strong factor is the "Precautionary Principle" in environmental regulation. This principle disallows an action that might harm the environment until the action is certain to be environmentally harmless. It is antithetical to science in practice, because it sets the impossible goal of proving harmlessness with certainty. In addition, a policy of "doing something" is promoted as "insurance" against possible risk to the earth. This idea of insurance as a prudent hedge is wrong on two counts, notwithstanding the lack of scientific evidence of significant humanmade warming. First, the actuarial notion of insurance is that of a carefully calculated premium, paid against a reasonably well-known risk in outcome and probability of outcome. But in the case of human-made global effects, the risk, premium, and outcomes cannot be well-defined. Second, the notion that implementing the Kyoto Protocol is effective insurance ignores the fact that the actual averted warming that would result is inconsequential. Indeed, the underlying basis for current international negotiations is the Rio Treaty of 1992, which specifically states that concentrations of greenhouse gases in the atmosphere, not emissions, be stabilized. In order to stabilize the air's concentration of greenhouse gases, emissions would have to be cut some 60 to 80 percent.

For the next several decades, fossil fuels are key to maintaining Americans' way of life and improving the human condition. According to the scientific facts as we know them today, there is no environmental reason we should not continue using them.

Steven Hayward

The Unheavenly Suburb: Understanding the Controversy over Urban Sprawl

Sprawl, in sum, is the new language of environmentalism.
—*New York Times*, February 6, 1999, A1

We must not overlook the fact that the market has, on the whole, guided the evolution of cities more successfully, though imperfectly, than is commonly realized and that most proposals to improve upon this, not by making it work better, but by superimposing a system of central direction, show little awareness of what such a system would have to accomplish, even to equal the market in effectiveness.

—F. A. Hayek, *The Constitution of Liberty,* p. 342

The debate over urban sprawl in America often masquerades as a public policy dispute over technical questions about urban planning, traffic congestion, mass transit, density, open space, and other aspects of urban form. But ultimately it is a debate about the nature of the good life in an affluent democracy—a debate representing a clash of community values and visions for our urban future.

The chief focus of this debate is the suburb, that unique form of city life that represents the confluence of modern prosperity and modern liberalism. A person who is not part of a city, Aristotle reminds us, "must therefore be either a beast or a god," because the first purpose of a city is to make possible the self-sufficiency of the household. It was not possible in antiquity to be self-sufficient without association with a city of some kind, and typically this meant, up until the early twentieth century, living in or very near central cities in very high population densities. Modern technology and prosperity enabled the suburban form of life, allowing citizens to live in comfort partially or wholly detached from the life and politics of the urban core. And modern (that is to say, eighteenth century) liberalism gave sanction to the enhanced sense of privacy and individuality that is the hallmark of suburban life. Because of this, modern cities find themselves in circumstances utterly unimaginable to Aristotle or any other early theorist on civil life. The central city no longer dominates.

This is exactly what contemporary communitarians of all stripes dislike about suburban sprawl, and it intersects neatly with the hatred environmentalists hold for the attributes of human prosperity and technology (especially the automobile), giving us the potent movement to reshape America known as "smart growth." Smart growth is a shrewd act of rhetorical labeling. Maryland Governor Parris Glendening is thought to have been the first politician to use the term, the first to make smart growth part of his policy agenda. It has caught on like wildfire; half of the nation's governors, from both parties, have embraced smart growth or an equivalent concept. The smart growth label puts potential critics on the defensive. Who, except for a cloddish developer, could possibly be for "dumb growth"? Indeed, even cloddish developers have embraced smart growth; the National Association of Home Builders, whose members will bear the brunt of any new smart growth regulations, has publicly endorsed smart growth and is laboring to refine the meaning of the term.

Smart growth supporters push a few core concepts that can be summarized as:

- Infrastructure projects (public works, such as roads, sewers, water mains, and schools) should be more carefully "targeted" so that they will be more "efficient." In practice, this means less infrastructure.

- New development should be more "transit oriented," with provision for light rail lines or bus routes.
- Development should be more "compact," or built to higher densities than is typical of suburban development today, partly to accommodate the proposed transit.
- Urban growth boundaries, a defined circumference around existing urban areas beyond which no development is allowed, could be employed (there is less unanimity on this point).

All of these features require "better planning" or "comprehensive planning," which some smart growth advocates say can only be accomplished with a powerful regional government.

Before we examine some of the problems with the smart growth plan for controlling sprawl, it is worth acknowledging that there is much in the smart growth concept that has merit. Indeed, its appeal cuts across ideological lines, as the aforementioned embrace by governors of both parties indicates. Although liberals and environmentalists have taken the lead in promoting smart growth, many conservatives agree with a number of its precepts. No one loves a strip mall, even though they are convenient. Indeed, many conservatives have embraced the neotraditional community design concepts of what is known as the "New Urbanism." Much of the smart growth critique could have come from the pen of Russell Kirk, while the rest of it could have come from Hayek and von Mises.

The most salient point of agreement is that neotraditional designs usually run afoul of zoning and planning regulations. Smart growth advocates often criticize rigid zoning and planning codes that prohibit mixed-use neighborhoods and stifle spontaneity in city design with the language of libertarianism. One of the most eloquent New Urbanist critics of modern planning, James Howard Kunstler, wrote in "Home From Nowhere" that:

Almost everywhere in the United States laws prohibit building the kinds of places that Americans themselves consider authentic and traditional. Laws prevent the building of places that human beings can feel good in and can afford to live in. Laws forbid us to build places that are worth caring about.

> Is Main Street your idea of a nice business district? Sorry, your zoning laws won't let you build it, or even extend it where it already exists. Is Elm Street your idea of a nice place to live— you know, houses with front porches on a tree-lined street? Sorry, Elm Street cannot be assembled under the rules of large-lot zoning and modern traffic engineering.[1]

Andres Duany, one of the leading New Urbanist architects, notes:

> Even the classic American main street, with its mixed-use buildings right up against the sidewalk, is now illegal in most municipalities. Somewhere along the way, through a series of small and well-intentioned steps, traditional towns became a crime in America.[2]

To the extent that the smart growth advocates recognize the ill effects of too much regulation and overzealous planning, it is vindication of Jane Jacobs' great 1961 analysis, *The Death and Life of Great American Cities*.[3] Jacobs, the preeminent critic of modern urban planning, could see that the centralized planning at the core of the new and fashionable policy to spark "urban renewal" was going to be a disaster. This approach taught that human activity needed to be isolated into zones (residential, industrial, commercial, and even recreational). Jacobs argued that cities and neighborhoods were a spontaneous order in exactly the way Austrian economists such as Hayek and von Mises understood it, which excessive planning and regulation would only disrupt for the worse.

At the time, Jacobs' book was very controversial among planners and urban politicians, who mostly brushed her aside as a gadfly. One of her early fans, however, was William F. Buckley, Jr., who included a chapter from *The Death and Life* in the first edition of the anthology *American Conservative Thought in the Twentieth Century* in 1970.[4] And before Jacobs, conservatives from as far back as the 1950s have criticized the interstate highway system for the effects it would have on life in rural towns bypassed by vehicle traffic, as well as the effect on interstate highways and urban expressways would have on big city neighborhoods.

While conservatives agree with some criticisms of sprawl, back in the 1960s some liberals actually worried that America was not sprawling enough. In 1967, *U.S. News and World Report* covered an interagency task force of the Johnson administration that sought to stave off overurbanization, or higher population density, in the cities.[5] The time has come, Agriculture Secretary Orville Freeman said, "to take issue with the urbanist school that believes the megalopolis is the wave of the future, with the countryside being preserved as a kind of huge national park where urbanites rest their nerves before plunging once again into the maelstrom of the city." We needed more exurban and rural development, they thought. If nothing was done, the Johnson Administration warned, by the year 2000, 208 million people would be "jammed" into cities on 3 percent of the U.S. land area—in fact, just about where we are today.[6] For liberals in the mid-1960s, this would be too much density; ironically, for the liberals of the smart growth movement of today, it is not enough.

Yet conservatives and libertarians find it hard to be card-carrying members of the smart growth movement. Although the smart growth critique offers sensible sound bytes about reducing planning and zoning regulations and allowing the market to work, in practice the smart growth agenda is highly prescriptive. With its emphasis on such techniques as "targeting" infrastructure, drawing urban growth boundaries, and creating regional governments, smart growth policy would require more centralized power and a planning prowess that greatly exceeds the scope of existing urban planning. The humility that one might naturally expect after recognizing the planning errors of the past is absent from most smart growth enthusiasts.

One can see this in the fact that many smart growth advocates now champion Jane Jacobs as a hero and leading light for their cause. In the words of one of Portland's regional planners, "A lot of us got tired of protesting the Vietnam War, read Jane Jacobs, and decided to take over Portland."[7] Such planners have read Jacobs either selectively or uncomprehendingly, for her central point was that well-functioning cities evolve spontaneously, beyond the reach of planners. Indeed, what might be called the latter-day "Jacobins" of smart growth have more in common with the eighteenth-century

variety of urban planner than they do with Jacobs. And Jacobs herself explicitly warned against trying to apply her urban insights to
suburban settings:

> I hope no reader will try to transfer my observations into guides
> as to what goes on in towns, or little cities, or in suburbs which
> still are suburban. Towns, suburbs and even little cities are
> totally different organisms from great cities. We are in enough
> trouble already from trying to understand big cities in terms of
> the behavior, and imagined behavior, of towns. To try to
> understand towns in terms of big cities will only compound
> confusion.[8]

Kunstler offers a maddening illustration of the contradictory
nature of the premises of the smart growth critique of planning
and zoning. First, he writes "if you want to make your community
better, begin at once by throwing out your zoning laws. Don't revise
them—get rid of them. Set them on fire if possible and make a
public ceremony of it. . . . While you're at it, throw out your 'master
plan' too. It's invariably just as bad." Most conservatives could stand
up and cheer at this, but Kunstler's next sentence undoes much of
the good of the antecedent. He continues: "Replace these things
with a traditional town-planning ordinance that prescribes a more
desirable everyday environment."[9] Note that troublesome word
"prescribe." Most smart growth enthusiasts are more than willing
to mandate their prescriptions on all of us through the power of
government. Before long it is possible to see in this issue the disas-
trous combination of utopian sentimentalism and the tyrannical
impulse of the modern administrative state.

At its root is a deep disaffection or even contempt for the lives
of ordinary suburban middle-class Americans. One of the most in-
famous descriptions came from Lewis Mumford's epic 1961 work,
The City in History, where he wrote that suburbs are

> a multitude of uniform, unidentifiable houses, lined up inflex-
> ibly, at uniform distances, on uniform roads, in a treeless com-
> munal waste, inhabited by people of the same class, the same

income, the same age group, witnessing the same television performances, eating the same tasteless pre-fabricated foods, from the same freezers, conforming in every outward and inward respect to a common mold, manufactured in the central metropolis. Thus the ultimate effect of the suburban escape is, ironically, a low-grade uniform environment from which escape is impossible.[10]

This is not a new attitude toward the suburbs. It was perhaps best captured by Herbert Gans in his well-known 1967 book, *The Levittowners*. Gans set out to study life in the post–World War II suburbs of tract homes, because, in his words, elite opinion regarded suburbanites as

> an uneducated, gullible, petty "mass" which rejects the culture that would make it fully human, the "good government" that would create the better community, and the proper planning that would do away with the landscape-despoiling little "boxes" in which they live.[11]

That attitude reflects the views of the smart growth elite today. In an overheated speech to the Congress for the New Urbanism in June 1999, Kunstler let loose his antisuburban rhetoric:

> It is the dwelling place of untruth. We call it suburbia. A cartoon of rural life, with none of the qualities of it. I believe we in the CNU [Congress for the New Urbanism] recognize its profound culturally toxic nature. . . . The common complaint about these brand-new mega-suburbs is that "everything looks the same." This is only the most superficial symptom of their evil nature. . . . Its present is a dangerously provisional collective hallucination, nourished by a sado-masochistic idiot pop culture, which can fall apart at the slightest provocation. We have a name for this collective hallucination, by the way: The American Dream, a sort of mega-lie stating that this sort of ghastly provisional collective hallucination is the ultimate state of being worth aspiring to.[12]

In a speech to the National League of Historic Theaters in 1999, Kunstler calls the suburbs "the national car slum," and derides the view that suburbs represent the outcome of the free choice of families as "arguments so dumb they're not worth debating."[13]

Nor is Kunstler an extreme or unusual example. Richard Moe of the National Trust for Historic Preservation calls sprawl, among other things, "socially irresponsible."[14] David Rusk conceived a fable in which sprawl was the evil means by which a foreign enemy went about destroying America's cities.[15] Urban affairs writer Neal Pierce has called suburban sprawl "a virus eating us from the inside out."[16] Andres Duany wrote that "suburban sprawl is a cancerous growth rather than healthy growth. . . . The suburb is the last word in privatization, perhaps even its lethal consummation, and it spells the end of authentic civic life."[17]

Suburban sprawl is now the all-purpose scapegoat for our urban discontents. Sprawl has even been blamed for the rise in obesity (Americans drive instead of walk) and as a contributing factor in the Columbine High School shootings (disconnected auto-dependent housing tracts and impersonal suburban malls generate violent "alienation" among youth).[18] If sprawl can be implicated as a primary cause in these matters, there is very little that cannot be attached to it. The poet Randall Jarrell is supposed to have remarked that we could solve most of our social problems "if only we could get our hands on this fellow 'Society.'" Today, "sprawl" seems to have become a substitute for "society" as the general cause of all bad things.

The great urban scholar Edward Banfield once offered the sober counsel that for urban problems, "Feasible measures are few and unsatisfactory as compared to what it would be nice to have happen or what one would do if one were dictator."[19] There are signs that many smart growth advocates, given political power, would not hesitate to engage in unlimited social engineering to make us all better people. At their frothiest, New Urbanists sound not unlike the Swedish social engineers of the 1960s and 1970s, who had no hesitation about using housing policy and planning regulations for the purpose of properly "socializing" Swedish citizens.

In his magisterial 1998 book, *Cities in Civilization*, Sir Peter Hall recounts just how looney the Swedish Social Democrats were in their heyday. He cites Lennart Holm, director general of the Directorate of National Planning in the 1970s, who said: "Estates of small houses are bad. They encourage social stratification, and this is what we want to avoid. . . . We cannot allow this to continue. . . . We cannot allow people to preserve their differences. People will have to give up the right to choose their own neighbors." Jan Stromdahl, architect with the Directorate, echoed this view: "I am afraid of living in a detached house, because it causes isolation, and restricts contact. I am interested in collective living, and want to see it spread." For full disclosure, few can top Ingrid Jussil, town planning expert with the Ministry of the Interior and a Social Democratic Party ideologist: "Town planning must emphasize the collective. We can achieve this by breaking down barriers, and forcing people into contact with each other. In that way, we can, for example, socialize children early. Society has got to decide how children are going to live."[20]

The eminent American political scientist Hugh Heclo stated:

> To the Social Democrats, housing policy was essentially a question of deciding what kinds of citizen the policy should help produce. As emphasized by one leading party official, homeownership in any form threatened to make Swedes preoccupied with their own private concerns. . . . Politically they fear—and their fears were realized in 1976—that a suburban Sweden would become a bourgeois Sweden with a bourgeois government.[21]

This kind of tyrannical impulse finds its echoes among smart growth advocates in the U.S. today, and constitutes the chief reason why conservatives and libertarians need to be wary of the movement. Hence, having acknowledged that some of the smart growth critique of suburban form has validity, it is necessary in the current climate of opinion to rally to the defense of suburbs. It has hardly been done better or more succinctly than by Herbert Gans in *The Levittowners*:

> The [suburban] community may displease the professional city planner and the intellectual defender of cosmopolitan culture,

but perhaps more than any other type of community, Levittown permits most of its residents to be what they want to be—to center their lives around the home and the family, to be among neighbors whom they can trust, to find friends to share their leisure hours, and to participate in organizations that provide sociability and the opportunity to be of service to others.[22]

Stepping down from the social and political dimension of the issue, there are narrower policy questions starting with whether our suburban discontents owe their origin to "market failure" in land use. Even Friedrich Hayek admits that that can be. "In many respects," Hayek wrote, "the close contiguity of city life invalidates any simple division of property rights. In such conditions it is true only to a limited extent that whatever an owner does with his property will affect only him and nobody else. What economists call the 'neighborhood effects,' i.e., the effects of what one does to one's property on that of others, assume major importance."[23]

However, even if one grants the propensity for market failure in land use, it does not immediately follow that land use market failure is readily corrected or prevented through "long range comprehensive planning." Agricultural economist Bruce Benson has written that "government regulation [of land use] appears to be creating more externalities than it prevents. . . . This 'government failure' may in fact be more costly to society than any market failure."[24] This is not to say that nothing can or should be done. Rather, as Hayek frames it, "the issue is not whether one ought or ought not to be for town planning but whether the measures to be used are to supplement and assist the market or to suspend it and put central direction in its place." Hence the one thing most needful in designing a growth management policy is to understand the ways in which urban planning, which seems on the surface a relatively simple, one-dimensional problem, shares the same difficulties as those of any other kind of centralized economic planning. The purpose of this discussion is, as Hayek suggests in the epigram to this essay, to gain an "awareness of what such a system would have to accomplish" to be effective.[25]

Much of the difficulty of comprehensive land use planning derives from a basic confusion about its two main constituent tasks: land classification and resource allocation. As a technical task, land classification is relatively simple. Allocating land resources through planning is another thing altogether. Planners, however, have come to think that because the first task—land classification—is simple and practical, the second task—allocating land resources—should be simple and practical as well. But the resource allocation task is inherently impossible to conquer because of what economists call the "knowledge" or "information problem." As economist E. C. Pasour, Jr., puts it: "The theoretical basis of land use planning is deficient in that no way has been found to solve the information problems inherent in all central economic planning. . . . [I]nformation problems have received relatively little attention in land use planning literature."[26]

This is not to say that nothing can or should be done. Rather, as Hayek frames it, "the issue is not whether one ought or ought not to be for town planning but whether the measures to be used are to supplement and assist the market or to suspend it and put central direction in its place."[27] Urban planning scholars Harry Richardson and Peter Gordon concur: "The proper role for planners is to strengthen markets and even create them. This risks of monopoly power reside much more in government institutions than in market. . . . Any claims for the cost of market failure [in land use] have to be balanced by an assessment of the costs of government failure . . . imperfect markets work better than imperfect government."[28] Sociologist Herbert Gans agrees: "Unlike city hall, the marketplace is sensitive to diversities among customers and does not require them to engage in political conflict to get what they want."[29]

When one ponders taking the smart growth critique of government land use regulation seriously, its central irony becomes evident.

While restrictive land use regulations should certainly be removed to allow for diversity in development, it is crucial to recognize that these regulations were implemented in response to the conventional wisdom about how development should take place. The conventional wisdom 30 years ago, for example, was that mixed use led to ugliness, conflict, and inefficiency; housing and commerce should be strictly segregated to prevent ruinous combinations. Now the conventional wisdom of smart growth holds just the reverse. We would commit the equal and opposite error if we removed regulations that prevent "new urban" forms and replaced them with new regulations that compel new urban forms. Better to let the marketplace respond to the preferences of real people than to substitute one erroneous conventional wisdom for another.

Notes

[1] James Howard Kunstler, "Home From Nowhere," *The Atlantic Monthly,* September 1996 <www.theatlantic.com/issues/96sep/kunstler/kunstler.htm>.

[2] Andres Duany, Elizabeth Plater-Zyberkn, and Jeff Speck, *Suburban Nation: The Rise of Sprawl and the Decline of the American Dream* (New York: North Point Press, 2000), p. xi.

[3] Jane Jacobs, *The Death and Life of Great American Cities* (New York: Random House, 1961). *Death and Life* is in its 14th printing.

[4] William F. Buckley, Jr., Ed., *American Conservative Thought in the Twentieth Century* (New York: Bobbs-Merrill, 1970).

[5] "Open Spaces Get Wider, Cities Grow Denser," *U.S. News and World Report* (December 18, 1967): 47.

[6] Ibid.

[7] For a splendid account of the smart growth misappropriation of Jacobs, see Jesse Walker, "Jacobean Tragedy," *Reason* (July 1998), available at <www.reason.com/9807/col.walker.html>.

[8] Jacobs, *The Death and Life of Great American Cities*, p. 16.

[9] Kunstler, "Home from Nowhere."

[10] Lewis Mumford, *The City in History* (New York: Harcourt, Brace and World, 1961), p. 486.

[11] Herbert Gans, *The Levittowners: Ways of Life and Politics in a New Suburban Community* (New York: Alfred A. Knopf, 1967), p. vi.

[12] James Howard Kunstler, "Reflections on the Columbine School Massacre," speech to the Congress for the New Urbanism, Milwaukee, June 6, 1999. Undated remarks from a copy on file with author.

[13] James Howard Kunstler, remarks made to the National League of Historic Theaters at the Allegro Hotel, Chicago, 1999. On file with author.

[14] Richard Moe, speech to San Joaquin Valley Town Hall, Fresno, California, November 20, 1996.

[15] David Rusk, *Inside Game, Outside Game: Winning Strategies for Saving Urban America* (Washington, D.C.: Brookings Institution Press, 2001), pp. 82–86.

[16]Neal R. Pierce, "Sprawling Problem," *Washington Times* (April 3, 1996): A2.

[17]Cited in William Schneider, "The Suburban Century Begins," *Atlantic Monthly* (July 1992): 37.

[18]Neal R. Pierce, "Littleton's Legacy: Our Suburban Dream Shattered," *Washington Post* (June 6, 1999).

[19]Edward Banfield, *The Unheavenly City Revisited* (Boston: Little, Brown, 1974), p. 269.

[20]Peter Hall in *Cities in Civilization* (New York: Pantheon, 1998), pp. 882–993.

[21]Hugo Heclo in *Cities in Civilization* (New York: Pantheon, 1998), p. 882.

[22]Gans, *The Levittowners*, pp. 412–13.

[23]F. A. Hayek, "Housing and Town Planning," *The Constitution of Liberty* (University of Chicago Press, 1961), p. 341.

[24]Bruce L. Benson, "Land Use Regulation: A Supply and Demand Analysis of Changing Property Rights," *Journal of Libertarian Studies* (Fall 1981): 449.

[25]Hayek, "Housing and Town Planning," *The Constitution of Liberty*, p. 342.

[26]E. C. Pasour, Jr., "Land Use Planning: Implications of the Economic Calculation Debate," paper presented to the Political Economy Research Center, Bozeman, Montana, December 1981.

[27]Hayek, "Housing and Town Planning," *The Constitution of Liberty*, p. 341.

[28]Harry W. Richardson and Peter Gordon, "Market Planning: Oxymoron or Common Sense?" *Journal of the American Planning Association* (Summer 1993): 347.

[29]Gans, *The Levittowners*, p. 416.

Appendix A
The New Urbanist Ahwahnee Principles

Preamble

Existing patterns of urban and suburban development seriously impair our quality of life. The symptoms are: more congestion and air pollution resulting from our increased dependence on automobiles, the loss of precious open space, the need for costly improvements to roads and public services, the inequitable distribution of economic resources, and the loss of a sense of community. By drawing upon the best from the past and the present, we can plan communities that will more successfully serve the needs of those who live and work within them. Such planning should adhere to certain fundamental principles.

Community Principles

1. All planning should be in the form of complete and integrated communities containing housing, shops, work places, schools, parks, and civic facilities essential to the daily life of the residents.
2. Community size should be designed so that housing, jobs, daily needs, and other activities are within easy walking distance of each other.
3. As many activities as possible should be located within easy walking distance of transit stops.
4. A community should contain a diversity of housing types to enable citizens from a wide range of economic levels and age groups to live within its boundaries.
5. Businesses within the community should provide a range of job types for the community's residents.
6. The location and character of the community should be consistent with a larger transit network.
7. The community should have a center focus that combines commercial, civic, cultural, and recreational uses.
8. The community should contain an ample supply of specialized open space in the form of squares, greens, and parks whose frequent use is encouraged through placement and design.
9. Public spaces should be designed to encourage the attention and presence of people at all hours of the day and night.
10. Each community or cluster of communities should have a well-defined edge, such as agricultural greenbelts or wildlife corridors, permanently protected from development.
11. Streets, pedestrian paths, and bike paths should contribute to a system of fully connected and interesting routes to all destinations. Their design should encourage pedestrian and bicycle use by being small and spatially defined by buildings, trees, and lighting, and by discouraging high-speed traffic.
12. Wherever possible, the natural terrain, drainage, and vegetation of the community should be preserved with superior examples contained within parks or greenbelts.

13. The community design should help conserve resources and minimize waste.
14. Communities should provide for the efficient use of water through the use of natural drainage, drought tolerant landscaping, and recycling.
15. The street orientation, the placement of buildings, and the use of shading should contribute to the energy efficiency of the community.

Regional Principles

1. The regional land-use planning structure should be integrated within a larger transportation network built around transit rather than freeways.
2. Regions should be bounded by and provide a continuous system of greenbelt/wildlife corridors to be determined by natural conditions.
3. Regional institutions and services (government, stadiums, museums, etc.) should be located in the urban core.
4. Materials and methods of construction should be specific to the region, exhibiting a continuity of history and culture and compatibility with the climate to encourage the development of local character and community identity.

Implementation Principles

1. The general plan should be updated to incorporate the above principles.
2. Rather than allowing developer-initiated, piecemeal development, local governments should take charge of the planning process. General plans should designate where new growth, infill, or redevelopment will be allowed to occur.
3. Prior to any development, a specific plan should be prepared based on these planning principles.
4. Plans should be developed through an open process and participants in the process should be provided visual models of all planning proposals.

<www.LGC.org/Ahwahnee/principles.html>

Appendix B
The Lone Mountain Compact:
Principles for Preserving Freedom and
Livability in America's Cities and Suburbs

The phenomenon of urban sprawl has become a preeminent controversy throughout the United States. Recently a number of scholars and writers, gathered at a conference about the issue at Lone Mountain Ranch in Big Sky, Montana, by the Political Economy Research Center, decided to distill their conclusions into the following brief statement of principles. The authors have called this statement the "Lone Mountain Compact," and have invited other writers and scholars to join in endorsing its principles.

Preamble

The unprecedented increase in prosperity over the last 25 years has created a large and growing upper middle class in America. New modes of work and leisure combined with population growth have fueled successive waves of suburban expansion in the twentieth century. Technological progress is likely to increase housing choice and community diversity even further in the twenty-first century, enabling more people to live and work outside the conventional urban forms of our time. These choices will likely include low-density, medium-density, and high-density urban forms. This growth brings rapid change to our communities, often with negative side effects, such as traffic congestion, crowded public schools, and the loss of familiar open space. All of these factors are bound up in the controversy that goes by the term "sprawl." The heightened public concern over the character of our cities and suburbs is a healthy expression of citizen demand for solutions that are responsive to our changing needs and wants. Yet trade-offs between different policy options for addressing these concerns are poorly understood. Productive solutions to public concerns will adhere to the following fundamental principles.

Principles for Livable Cities

The most fundamental principle is that, absent a material threat to other individuals or the community, people should be allowed to live and work where and how they like.

Prescriptive, centralized plans that attempt to determine the detailed outcome of community form and function should be avoided. Such "comprehensive" plans interfere with the dynamic, adaptive, and evolutionary nature of neighborhoods and cities.

Densities and land uses should be market driven, not plan driven. Proposals to supersede market-driven land use decisions by centrally directed decisions are vulnerable to the same kind of perverse consequences as any other kind of centrally planned resource allocation decisions, and show little awareness of what such a system would have to accomplish even to equal the market in effectiveness.

Communities should allow a diversity in neighborhood design, as desired by the market. Planning and zoning codes and building regulations should allow for neotraditional neighborhood design, historic neighborhood renovation and conversion, and other mixed-use development and the more decentralized development forms of recent years.

Decisions about neighborhood development should be decentralized as far as possible. Local neighborhood associations and private covenants are superior to centralized or regional government planning agencies.

Local planning procedures and tools should incorporate private property rights as a fundamental element of development control. Problems of incompatible or conflicting land uses will be better resolved through the revival of common law principles of nuisance than through zoning regulations which tend to be rigid and inefficient.

All growth management policies should be evaluated according to their cost of living and "burden-shifting" effects. Urban growth boundaries, minimum lot sizes, restrictions on housing development, restrictions on commercial development, and other limits on freely functioning land markets that increase the burdens on lower income groups must be rejected.

Market-oriented transportation strategies should be employed, such as peak period road pricing, HOT lanes, toll roads, and de-monopolized mass transit. Monopoly public transit schemes, especially fixed rail transit that lacks the flexibility to adapt to the changing destinations of a dynamic, decentralized metropolis, should be viewed skeptically.

The rights of present residents should not supersede those of future residents. Planners, citizens, and local officials should recognize that "efficient" land use must include consideration for household and consumer wants, preferences, and desires. Thus, growth controls and land-use planning must consider the desires of future residents and generations, not solely current residents.

Planning decisions should be based upon facts, not perceptions. A number of the concerns raised in the "sprawl" debate are based upon false perceptions. The use of good data in public policy is crucial to the continued progress of American cities and the social advance of all its citizens.

For more information and background on these principles, see *A Guide to Smart Growth: Shattering Myths, Providing Solutions*, edited by Jane S. Shaw and Ronald D. Utt (Washington, D.C.: PERC/Heritage Foundation, 2000).

<www.PERC.org/publications/articles/lone_mountain_full.html>

MALCOLM WALLOP

Is This Land Our Land?
Federal vs. Private Land Ownership

I begin with a dark tale. One early morning in October of 1992, California rancher Donald Scott awoke to the sounds of a break-in in his house. Arming himself with a pistol and accompanied by his wife, Frances, he moved to confront the black-clad intruders, hoods masking their features. He was shot dead by what turned out to have been members of the Los Angeles County Sheriff's Department. Accompanied by the DEA and armed officers of the Forest Service and the National Park Service, they invaded the Scott home on the pretext that he was cultivating marijuana in baskets hanging from a tree. They claimed the plants had been sighted from an airplane flying at 1,000 feet. In the end, nothing was found in his house and no marijuana plants or drugs of any kind were found on his ranch. Obviously, something else was going on here. According to author Michael Fesser, Jr., writing in the *Los Angeles Times Magazine:*

> In fact, the "something else" turned out to be nothing less than "the land itself," no less an inalienable right than private property, a citizen's right to security in his own home. Scott's death in the doorway of his own bedroom would become a central provocation in the controversy over the fairness—some would say the constitutionality—of federal and state asset-forfeiture statutes, which allow authorities to confiscate cash, goods or real estate that they can connect with drug trafficking and other crimes.[1]

Mrs. Scott took things a step further. Every chance she got she called her husband's death "premeditated," and she called it "murder." "They (the agencies) knew we were getting ready to sell the land, and they had to escalate their maneuvers to acquire it," she told the *Malibu Surftide News*. "I believe they deliberately killed Donald." She fingered the National Park Service, the Scotts' property neighbor on three sides, as a "major coconspirator."

In truth, whether it was the National Park Service, who, unwilling to pay for the land for the Santa Monica Mountains National Recreation Area, chose the Racketeer Influenced and Corrupt Organizations Act (RICO) to seize it, or whether it was one of many other agencies matters little. They all fought over the spoils.

This tale is chilling, yet it is far from unique. The 1970s RICO act was designed to fight the Mafia and drug lords; now it is one of the principle means that governments at all levels—federal, state, and local—can use to seize what they want without the complications of the 5th Amendment's requirement of just compensation.

No member of the Park Service nor any police officer was ever punished for this—call it what it was—murder for public convenience. Frances Scott sued the sheriff's department and was eventually awarded $4 million. Although it was the largest award in Los Angeles County history, it can be of little comfort.

In today's America, government at all levels can use any means from RICO to regulatory agencies—such as those designed to administer banks or the environment or worker safety—to impose anything from bankruptcy, to prison, and even death to coerce acquiescence from what they like to call "willing sellers." Asset forfeiture provisions, at the very least, force surrender negotiations for all but the most courageous and well-heeled. Asset forfeiture is the tool of rulers, not representatives.

Is this land our land, and does government own or desire too much? Indeed, does it matter how much government owns? Who is the new elite who would dispossess our citizens? Do we possess the tools to reverse or stem this tide? Can states or courts or citizens resist? Why should they?

Our courts are just beginning to condemn, on occasion, these outrageous assaults on ordinary Americans. It is important to note that it is not just the rich whose property rights are threatened. Anyone who confronts the power of bureaucrats can find himself fighting for his family, his property, and even his life in a land whose fundamental founding premise was the right to own property.

Protecting the rights of private property owners was of utmost importance to the Founding Fathers as they drafted the Declaration of Independence and the Constitution. They fought the Revolutionary War to protect those rights. "Liberty, property and no stamps!" was the first slogan of the American Revolution. According to Catherine Drinker Bowen: ". . . property was not a privilege of the higher orders but a right which everyone fought to defend."[2]

In *Federalist,* no. 79, Alexander Hamilton wrote: "A power over a man's subsistence amounts to a power over his will."

John Adams wrote similarly: "the moment that idea is admitted into society that property is not as sacred as the Laws of God, and that there is not a force of law and public justice to protect it, anarchy and tyranny commence. Property must be sacred or liberty cannot exist."

Likewise Samuel Adams: "The Natural Rights of the colonists are these: first, a right to life; second, to liberty; third, to property; together with the right to support and defend them in the best manner they can."

James Madison understood that the protection of property was the foundation of all freedoms: "In a word, as a man is said to have a right to his property, he may be equally said to have a property in his rights. Where an excess of power prevails, property of no sort is duly respected. No man is safe in his opinions, his person, his faculties, or his possessions. . . . Government is instituted to protect property of every sort. . . . This being the end of government, that alone is a *just* government, which *impartially* secures to every man, whatever is his *own.*"

These quotes refer to private property. When we speak of public lands, however, the specter of official greed comes into view. In examining the government's boundless appetite for public land, we must ask two questions. First, Is this land our land? And second, Does government own or desire too much?

To the first question the answer is that not enough of this land is our land. Government, on all levels, owns nearly 50 percent. Is that too much? Absolutely. Every acre the government owns is a burden on the owners of every private acre. The taxes paid on private property pay for police and fire protection, highways and roads, airports, hospitals, and schools. The so-called PILT (payment in lieu of taxes) does not cover the revenue demands created by public land ownership. Yet with every acre lost to government ownership, our tax base declines as our costs increase.

Kathy Stupak-Thrall owned a cabin on the shores of Michigan's Crooked Lake, adjacent to the Sylvania Wilderness Area. When the law that created that wilderness area was being discussed, congressional and Forest Service testimony assured everyone that valid existing rights would be respected and that motorized boating would continue. No sooner was the wilderness area established than the Forest Service forbade motorized boat access.

The damage this brought to the Stupak-Thralls and others who had commercial fishing camps was enormous, so they brought suit against the Forest Service to restore their rights. The courts initially sided with the Forest Service, causing Michigan Governor John Engler's office to issue the following comment in October 1996: "If the lower court decision remains intact, the Forest Service will have . . . carte blanche to issue similarly restrictive regulations that detrimentally affect Michigan residents who own property near or adjacent to federal wilderness areas."[3]

In the end, on appeal, the property owners' right to motorized boating was restored—but not until they had spent $300,000 in legal fees, and suffered incalculable losses in time and income.

Other Forest Service management practices, such as "controlled burns" in New Mexico in 1999 that resulted in massive private property losses of homes, are every bit as unprofessional. That a controlled burn was initiated in a drought during high wind warnings was unbelievable incompetence. Nevertheless, former Secretary of the Interior Bruce Babbitt blamed the homeowners for their losses: They should not have built their homes where they had.

The National Park Service presides over some of the most overgrazed, poorly managed lands in America. The Grand Canyon's burro population is destroying vegetation along the entire length of the canyon. In Yellowstone National Park, there are no willow breaks in alpine meadows, and aspen does not exist except in fenced enclosures: They were destroyed by the huge, unregulated herds of elk, buffalo, and other wildlife. Rather than manage its trust, the Park Service manages its politics. Too many interest groups have too much say as to what constitutes good policy, and that policy has become as changeable as the seasons.

In Yellowstone a few years ago it was decided to allow nature to hold sway. All previously managed assets were turned over to the forces of nature without appreciating, or understanding, that land that has been meticulously managed for a century could only be damaged in the extreme by a management policy not to manage. When wildfire consumed nearly 700,000 acres, we were told it was a good and natural thing. But soon thereafter, when a park visitor became enraged because a buffalo wandered onto thin ice and was allowed to drown in plain sight, natural selection was determined too harsh for the park.

The reason that this management confusion should concern us is clear. President Clinton created millions of acres of national monuments by executive order, thereby eroding the ability of that land to benefit the American people. One such monument, Grand Escalante Rising, has been consigned to totally restricted asset management status. Its mineral resources, which had once provided funds for schools and roads in Utah and Arizona, are no longer available. The energy that billions of tons of America's cleanest coal could have produced will be replaced by increased, and increasingly questionable, hydro dam development along the Colorado River. Utah and Arizona were not compensated for these losses, and America's environmental loss went unremarked.

In national forests and on Bureau of Land Management land, the Clinton Administration imposed uneconomic permitting procedures for access to water in Colorado that had been municipally owned since before the establishment of the Forest Service. Long established grazing rights became uneconomic under new fee structures. Ranches were forced to subdivide and sell their herds, and school tax bases began to disappear. Ranch hands were let go; they and their families became urban dwellers, and small towns grew even smaller.

At every level of government in every state, there are those who believe that the land is threatened by private ownership, and that it must be removed to the federal or local government estate. A varied menu of environmental laws, including the Endangered Species, Clean Water, and Clean Air acts are now tools for control or confiscation of property rather than for their professed purpose of protecting the environment. Administrative agencies such as the DEA and FDIC and FCC use regulations and authorities to fine, as well as to force asset forfeiture under RICO. The one thing they have in common is the desire to take without just compensation.

Former Secretary Babbitt once wrote that the "old Anglo-Saxon idea of lines on the ground is no longer an acceptable concept." In his view, government must have the say as to who owns what and how that property can be used. Today, we have many in both parties who agree with Bruce Babbitt's statement that "there is not enough money to satisfy the constitutional requirement that no property shall be taken for public purposes without just compensation." Think about that: What they are saying is that if it is in the national interest to seize or control a piece of property, then one American must afford what all Americans are said to be unable to afford.

Secretary Babbitt once claimed that the worst mistake the federal government ever made was to give the Western states control over their water. The Clean Water Act, however, helped him to correct that error. His reasoning is that if the federal government controls water, which is a property right, it controls the economic destiny of any state and the behavior of all men. That is a taking of property of unprecedented dimensions, and one which will largely go unnoticed. In the Klamath Valley of Oregon, in order to save a fish poisoned by the very Fish and Wildlife Service now seeking to save it, several hundred families who had paid for and been guaranteed water will now be denied that water—without compensation.

Those who assert that these claims are justified and proper have never owned this kind of property. And they would be offended in the extreme should anyone assert a claim on their condominiums or automobiles. They are joined by a scientific elite willing to lie to achieve its goals. Forest Service and Fish and Wildlife Service employees planted lynx hairs on rubbing posts to concoct an endangered species presence. These are the same people who fought to reestablish the wolf in Yellowstone Park, not because of its romantic presence and mournful howls, but because the wolf's introduction under the Endangered Species Act gave them territorial control over private holdings in "The Greater Yellowstone Eco-System."

The lynx presence, had the hoax involved gone undiscovered, would have provided restricted management over huge tracts of land in Washington and Oregon. These "scientists" and "experts" were willing to sacrifice integrity to attain power.

It is sad to say that other threats are rising. The U.S. Senate, without debate and with the anonymity of a voice vote, passed S.990 after its parent Conservation and Reinvestment Act (CARA) failed. This piece of work provides $600 million a year for five years in grants to states to acquire land and to fund the actions of the most aggressive environmental groups. In the words of the American Land Rights Association, "S.990 has NO protections or prohibitions against eminent domain," allowing land acquisition agents to threaten condemnation at their will. Private property can be condemned for a laundry list of reasons, including any area that is "adaptable as a feeding, resting, or breeding place for wildlife." Lock up your bird feeders! The most vague and dangerous excuse to seize land is that funds "shall be used to address the unmet needs for wildlife and the habitats on which the wildlife depend."[4]

The point of all of this is that with money, desire, and legal chicanery, anyone can be forced to become a "willing seller." Nor, if the states do the coercing—and they have shown themselves only too willing—is it in any way better than if the federal money that feeds them had been used to a federal end.

This bill, S.990, passed in the Senate without any consideration but political. Its potential invasion of property rights is real, and its additions to the government estate will be enormous.

When I was in the Senate, we tried on several occasions to ensure just compensation for federal takings in a property rights bill. But the Senate could not muster the courage to enact it for fear of "the cost." Senator Bob Dole, trying to be helpful, said he would be supportive if an individual were to lose over 30 percent of his economic value. But nowhere does our constitution contemplate fractionate loss before compensation is offered.

Some courts are now beginning to fight back against the worst property rights abuses, but the states can be powerfully aggressive, too. The problem is that the fight for established rights is beyond the means of most citizens: Few can afford to engage a combatant who has no financial or time constraints.

So how do we fight back? Some legal foundations have aided citizens in the courts. In addition, the Constitution gives us rights that too few of us—able lawyers included—know about. J. L. Tenney, the president of Frontiers of Freedom, has written compellingly about the "enclave clause":

> Although the Enclave Clause of the U.S. Constitution, article I, section 8, clause 17, authorizes Congress to purchase, own and control land within the boundary of a state, it is very specific and limiting as to what type of lands the federal government can own and control within a given state. It also leaves no doubt that the state legislature has to relinquish control of those lands. The relevant portion of the Enclave clause reads: "Congress may exercise exclusive legislative authority over all places purchased by the consent of the legislature of the state in which the same shall be, for the erection of forts, magazines, arsenals, dockyards, and other needful buildings.[5]

This clause calls into question whether any agency of the federal government may come into a state and purchase land without state authorization as any other buyer would. It also renders doubtful whether a property owner has a simple right to sell to the federal government. Had the Founding Fathers intended the federal government to have this authority, they would never have included the enclave provision in the Constitution. Had the people believed the Constitution would allow the federal government to acquire any land it desired and displace state authority, they would never have allowed their states to ratify the Constitution. Clearly, issues other than private property rights must have been at stake, and those issues must have been of sufficient gravity to compel the Founders to include this clause and for the people to accept it.

In the *Records of the Federal Convention*, we find a telling explanation of the enclave clause's wording: "Mr. Gerry contended that (the power of the Federal government to purchase lands within states) might be made use of to enslave any particular State by buying up its territory, and that the strongholds proposed would be a means of awing the State into an undue obedience to the Genl. Government. . . . Thus after the word 'purchased' the words 'by the consent of the Legislature of the State'" was added to the Enclave Clause.[6]

With the best of intentions, the Nature Conservancy has a policy of purchasing private property and then reselling it to the federal government, often without any state commentary. The net effect of this is to diminish a state or county's tax base, and subject adjacent property owners to a new set of required operations declared by its new federal neighbors. And it is important to keep in mind here that the U.S. Supreme Court ruled in *Kleppe* v. *New Mexico*, 426 U.S. 529, (1976), that Congress exercises "complete" jurisdiction over public lands.

Our Founding Fathers' revolutionary view was that property ownership is a fundamental right. Others have viewed property from a sinister opposing posture. In 1932 William Z. Foster, then national chairman of the Communist Party USA, restated point one of the "Communist Manifesto":"The abolition of private property." Then, in terms specifically applicable to the United States, Foster said, "The establishment of an American Soviet government will involve the confiscation of large landed estates in town and country, and also the whole body of forests, mineral deposits, lakes, rivers. . . ." And USA Communist Party Chief Gus Hall later wrote, "The battle will be lost, not when freedom of speech is finally taken away, but when Americans become so 'adjusted or conditioned' to getting along with the 'group' that when they finally see the threat, they say, 'I can't afford to be controversial.'"

Aside from the fact that government is a notoriously bad manager of property, the truth is that the more property that is in government hands, the less freedom Americans can exercise. Unlike virtually all of the rest of the world, freedom in America—according to America's founding principles—is not bestowed by government. Yet in practice today, roaming rights and recreational and industrial uses of land can be regulated or prohibited according to whimsy, for vengeful reasons, or, still worse, in the name of "popular" opinion. And this without just compensation.

If it becomes a given that we cannot count on owning what we acquire, then we cannot enjoy the fruits of our labor—except through obsequious accommodation to those who rule. In the last administration we witnessed the true manifestation of this kind of rule by fiat. Republicans who sought and failed to push through CARA and then succeeded with S.990 are no more reliable than those about whom they so loudly complain. Any agency that can, in an asset forfeiture raid, kill a man for his property and go unpunished, can find the means to make any of us "willing sellers." A Fish and Wildlife Service that will plant lynx hairs to create a false endangered species presence can regulate any one of us off our land. A State of Florida that will condemn property held in private hands for 90 years by claiming that the state sold it in error can make any one of us surrender, knowing that to contest is futile. An EPA that can, through the courts, reverse its approval to construct after construction has been completed can bankrupt any one of us without looking back.

These are warning signs that there are those who wish to rule rather than represent Americans. Once we are ruled, we will no longer be able to claim to be the land of the free and the home of the brave. It is up to us to recall Madison's argument that the right to property is essential to all other rights. It stands in the way of slavery. We must see that this will be never be our rate.

Notes

[1] Michael Fesser, Jr., *Los Angeles Times Magazine* (August 1, 1993).

[2] Catherine Drinker Bowen, *Miracle at Philadelphia* (Boston: Little, Brown & Co., 1986).

[3] The Office of the Governor, "Governor Engler Requests Amicus Brief for Upper Peninsula Lake Dispute with Feds," Press release, October 23, 1996.

[4] American Land Rights Association, "Crisis Alert: CARA Land Grab," December 20, 2001, <www.landrights.org>.

[5] Bill Howell and J. L. Tenney, "Federal Acquisition of Land with States," <www.allianceforamerica.org>.

[6] James Madison in the *Records of the Federal Convention*, September 5, 1787.

PETER FERRARA

The Social Security Debate, 2002

In 1924, Chile became the first nation in the Western hemisphere to adopt the traditional social security system.

In 1981, the revolution for social security reform began in Chile. That year, Chile's minister of labor—an economist who learned his economics at the University of Chicago—led the country to adopt a comprehensive personal account option for social security. At that time, the tax rate in Chile was high as 26 percent. Under the option, workers were allowed to put 10 percent in a personal investment account system (with another two or three percentage points used for private survivors and disability insurance). The workers could choose from a list of major investment firms that were approved by the government. Some of these were major American firms, such as Chase Manhattan Bank and State Street Global Advisors. Today there are rural farm workers walking the hills of rural Chile, wearing serapes and leading their burros behind them, who have Chase Manhattan Bank investing their money.

In fewer than two years, over 90 percent of Chilean workers chose the private account options. The amount that they are required to pay into the system is less than half that required in the old system. As a result, the average Chilean worker now has more savings than the average American worker, even though the average Chilean earns one-seventh as much as the average American. The country's savings rate has soared to over 25 percent, which has contributed greatly to the country's booming economic growth over the last 20 years.

Through the personal accounts, Chilean workers are rapidly achieving the old socialist dream of owning the nation's businesses and industry. But because they own it directly, rather than through the government, this is more accurately called worker capitalism. Chile's experience has been recognized as such a great economic and political success that countries across Latin America have adopted similar reforms. Today, seven other countries have already done so, including Argentina, Mexico, Peru, Colombia, Bolivia, Uruguay, and El Salvador.

The trend has now spread beyond Latin America. Great Britain began adopting a private option for social security over 20 years ago, which allows workers to opt out of over half of its complete system. Over 80 percent of its workers have exercised the option. The Organization for Economic Cooperation and Development (OECD) reports that as a result Britain enjoys substantial economic advantages over other Western European nations. In 1996, Australia began phasing in a personal account system that over time will replace the old government system, relegating it to a means-tested safety-net role. Singapore has had a sort of fully invested system—not really a personal account system, but an essential investment fund—for decades now.

More recently, the trend has spread to Eastern Europe. Hungary and the former Soviet Republic of Kazakhstan adopted personal account options for their workers in 1998; Poland did so in 1999. Remarkably, that great socialist haven Sweden now allows workers to put 2.5 percentage points of their social security tax into personal accounts. More remarkably, this personal account reform is well underway in both Russia and China.

In 1994, the World Bank globalized this trend with a 400-page report that thoroughly applauds the reform.[1] When I read it, I thought it had been cribbed from the Cato Institute. I was surprised at how thoroughly they had adopted the argument that was laid out in my first book, published in 1980 (which was Cato's first hardback book).[2] The World Bank labeled Chile's reform a great success that would work in all countries—developed, developing, undeveloped. The reform would have special benefits for lower income countries in helping to develop their economies.

Social Security Reform in the United States

A poll conducted in the early 1990s found that more than twice as many young adults believed in UFOs as believed that Social Security would exist by the time they retire.

In 1996, in an annual address to the American Economics Association, Martin Feldstein, the former Chairman of the Council of Economic Advisors, President of National Bureau of Economic Research, and Harvard economics professor, called for the privatization of Social Security through some kind of invested personal account system.[3] (His speech was later published in the *American Economic Review*.) Being the econometrician that he is, Feldstein calculated that the present discounted value of the net benefit to America of privatizing Social Security would be $10 to $20 trillion. Michael Tanner and I examined that number and concluded it was very conservative. But even $10 to $20 trillion would be a huge gain to the United States.

Pete DuPont first campaigned for president on Social Security reform, as did Steve Forbes. Numerous bills have appeared in Congress. Former California Assemblyman Howard Kaloogian was one of four people leading the effort for what I call "pension liberation" among state employees. This would give them the option to shift out of a traditional defined benefit plan into personal accounts and defined contribution plans.

In 2000, George Bush campaigned with Social Security reform in his platform. After the election, as promised, he established a bipartisan commission to develop Social Security reform proposals based on a personal account option. The commission was made up of seven Democrats and seven Republicans and was co-chaired by former Democratic Senator Daniel Patrick Moynihan, his party's Social Security expert, and AOL/Time Warner CEO Richard Parsons. The commission also included former Democratic Representative Tim Petty of Minnesota, Democratic economist Estelle James of the World Bank, and Olivia Mitchell of the Wharton School. The commission was staffed by experts from the Social Security Administration who did the number crunching. Among the commission's conclusions were:

- Social Security will be strengthened if modernized to include a system of voluntary personal accounts;
- personal accounts would permit individuals to seek a higher rate of return on their Social Security contributions, offering a higher total expected benefit to individuals with accounts, as compared to those not having accounts; and
- any properly structured personal account option should increase expected benefits for Social Security participants.

The commission's projections show that individuals who are given the opportunity to invest in personal accounts should expect increases in total benefits. Remember, this is the Social Security Administration talking. Retirement security would be increased through personal accounts because they would facilitate wealth creation for individual participants.

Then the commission developed three alternative reform plans. They all include well-designed personal accounts, which allow you to put two to four percentage points of Social Security payroll tax into a personal account. They include caps and phase-outs and other complications, but that is not what is important. What is important is that this establishment commission of Republicans and Democrats, staffed by the Social Security Commission, looked at personal accounts and concluded that they are viable and beneficial. As a result, the idea of personal accounts has gone establishment. Actually, the staff of the Social Security Administration had started working on this in 1997, supported by the Clinton administration. But Clinton went on to do other things, and not Social Security reform.

Reasons for Reform

There are five reasons why social security reform is sweeping the world. The first is the famous Social Security financing crisis in the U.S. When I started writing about this in 1979 and 1980, some very conservative people were saying that Social Security was in financial trouble—and the establishment was saying that this was nuts. By the mid-1980s, everyone was saying that the system had serious long-term financial problems. The latest annual report of the Social Security board of trustees said the system would run out of funds in 2038. Paying promised benefits to today's young workers after that time would require at least a 50 percent tax increase— from today's 12 percent payroll tax to 18 percent. Under more pessimistic assumptions, the payroll tax may need to be doubled to 24 percent. This is why those young adults believe in UFOs more than in Social Security. And they are right: They may never receive their currently promised benefits because those increased tax rates will be hard to bear.

In fact, Social Security's financial crisis will not occur when the trust funds run out. Its financial crisis will occur after the trust funds peak and start to decline, which will happen in 2016. At that time, the trust fund bonds will have to be turned in to the government to obtain the money to pay benefits. And 2016 is only 14 years away. Most of the money that is paid in to Social Security is immediately paid out in current benefits—85 to 90 percent. The remaining 10 percent historically has been lent to the federal government, which immediately spends it. In the last few years, it has been used to retire federal debt. In return, the federal government gives Social Security a bond. But because there are no assets backing the bond, it is, in reality, an I.O.U. When Social Security needs to redeem a bond, the federal government has to do something to get the money: either raise taxes, borrow and increase the national debt, or cut government expenditures. From 2016 to 2038, Social Security will be turning in $3 trillion in trust fund bonds. Where is the federal government going to get $3 trillion? That will be the beginning of the financial crisis.

Why will we have this crisis? It starts from the fact that Social Security is not an investment program. It doesn't save money. It doesn't invest money. When Social Security began 60 years ago, the agency wasn't sure what it was going to do—whether it was going to invest the money paid to it or not. The Administration soon realized that saved and invested funds would be compromised for years. They decided instead to start paying benefits immediately.

There are multiple other factors contributing to the crisis. When the baby boom generation begins to retire within a few years, the baby bust generation will comprise most of the workforce. A very large group will begin taking money out of the system at a time when a very small group will be paying money into it. And people are living longer. If there are no reserves and the system must rely on current taxes to pay benefits, the tax rate will have to go up. Unfortunately, wage growth has been slower during the last quarter century than was expected.

A shift to personal accounts would eliminate these problems entirely. An unfunded system would be replaced by a fully funded system, with complete and full reserves to finance the expected benefits. The unfunded liability of Social Security would be reduced to the extent that workers exercise the personal account option.

Funding crisis aside, what isn't often considered in all this is that Social Security benefits do not represent good financial planning. Even if the promised benefits can somehow be paid, the returns on workers' forced investments are very low.

In the beginning, as in any Ponzi scheme, Social Security was a good deal, because people were getting more out of the system than they had paid in. The very first official retiree of the Social Security system was Ida Fuller. She retired at age 65, after having paid $44 into the system. She lived to be 100, and drew $25,000 in benefits. But now the reverse is happening. Now people are retiring into a system that has no savings or investments, that earns no returns, and that operates by redistributing funds from one group to another as fast as possible.

For most young workers today, even if Social Security managed to pay them all the benefits promised, the real rate of return on the amount of taxes they will have paid over their careers would be around 1 percent or less. For many, it will be zero or even a negative. In fact, the last report of the president's commission says that "social security actuaries estimate that for a single male worker born in 2000 with average earnings, the real annual return on his currently scheduled contribution to social security will be only 0.86 percent."[4]

For workers who pay the maximum amount of tax, the real annual return is −0.72 percent. In contrast, the long-run real rate of return of the stock market after adjusting for inflation is 7.5 to 8 percent (that is, after inflation, depending on how you calculate it). The long-term real return on corporate bonds has been around 3 percent or more.

In *A New Deal for Social Security*, Michael Tanner and I illustrated what an important difference this makes.[5] A husband and wife enter the workforce in 1985, with the husband earning the average income for men and the wife earning the average income for women each year. They have two children. Suppose they can save and invest into personal accounts over their entire careers what they and their employers would otherwise have put into Social Security. (Funds for survivor benefits, disability benefits, and other costs were taken into account.) Suppose they earn a 4 percent real rate of return over that time. (Four percent is just over half the average return earned in the stock market over the last 75 years.) They would reach retirement age with a fund of about $1 million in today's dollars. That fund would pay them more out of continual returns alone than Social Security promises but cannot pay, allowing them to leave $1 million to their children. Or they could buy an annuity that would pay them over three times what Social Security promises. This is a conservative estimate of what average-income families are losing through the current unreformed Social Security system.

At a 6 percent real rate of return, which is still less than the average return earned in the stock market over the last 75 years, the couple would retire with $1.6 million in today's dollars. That fund would pay them about three times what is promised by Social Security, while allowing them to leave the entire $1.6 million to their children. Or it could finance an annuity paying them seven times what Social Security promises but cannot pay. We found the same results for workers of all income levels and family combinations: one-earner families, two-earner families, different income mixes. They all could have much higher benefits through the private account system than through Social Security. (Among the Web sites that can calculate outcomes for different earning scenarios are <www.socialsecurity.org> and <www.heritage.org>.)

In the current system, money paid in is immediately paid out to finance current beneficiaries. A fully funded invested system, on the other hand, creates new income and wealth every year through the personal accounts and through the capital investments made through the personal accounts. That is the second reason for reform.

The third reason is what I call the new progressivism. The top half of income earners have been riding the long-term capital market boom over the past 20 years through IRAs, 401Ks, stock options, and the like, but those in the lower half of income earners have been missing out. They do not have the funds to put aside for such investments. As a result, lower wage earners are falling further behind in both income and accumulation of wealth. The personal Social Security investment account option would give them the chance to participate in the capital markets as well. Wealth and income distribution would become far more equal. In fact, years ago Martin Feldstein did a study that found that by privatizing Social Security, the concentration of wealth would be reduced by 50 percent.

Of course, these lower income workers would also receive larger retirement checks. Michael Tanner and I discussed this in *A New Deal for Social Security*.[6] A husband and wife enter the workforce and earn basically the minimum wage over their entire careers. If they paid into a personal account system from the beginning, and earned just 4 percent real return on the investment, they would retire with a trust fund of about $375,000 in today's dollars, after inflation. And they could use that fund to buy an annuity that would pay about two and a half times what Social Security promises but cannot pay. At a 6 percent real return, which is still less than the average stock market return, the couple would retire with a trust fund of almost $700,000 in today's dollars. That fund could finance an annuity that would pay them about five times what Social Security promises but cannot pay. Indeed, the fund would pay more out of continued investment returns alone than Social Security promises, while allowing the couple to leave the fund of almost $700,000 to their children.

An interesting factor to consider is that Social Security is skewed by subsidy to favor lower income workers. What old-time stalwarts of the current system have a hard time accepting is that the higher benefits of the private system overwhelm those subsidies.

Another factor is that lower-income people have shorter life expectancies than higher-income people. They tend to have fewer years in which to collect retirement benefits. This is most true of African-Americans. A black male born today has a life expectancy of 64.8 years. The Social Security Administration has already scheduled the rise in retirement age to 67 years. This means that most black males born today will not receive any Social Security benefits—even though they will have paid into the system throughout their working lives.

The Heritage Foundation took the lower life expectancy of African-Americans into account in a ground-breaking study.[7] It found that the promised Social Security return for a low-income single black male age 30 today is −0.66 percent. This amounts to paying the bank to hold your money rather than the bank paying you interest. For an average-income 30-year-old single black male, the promised return is −1.5 percent. A two-earner, low-income black couple, each age 30, with two children, would receive a return of 1 percent. If that same couple earned an average income, the return would be 0 percent.

Personal accounts would eliminate these negative effects for African-Americans. And those who die before retirement age can leave their account funds to their families.

Low-income workers bear the brunt of the current system's benefit cuts and tax increases. Consequently, they would benefit most by a move to an alternative system.

There are two other reasons the reform system is preferable. One is economic growth. Increasing the savings investment in our country through personal accounts would increase capital investment, increase productivity, and increase wages, jobs, and economic growth over time, as well as reducing payroll taxes. People will not need to pay as much into their personal accounts as they pay into the current Social Security system because the returns on the personal accounts will be so much higher.

The fifth reason the personal account system is preferable to the current Social Security system is freedom of choice. Individuals will have more control over their money. They will be able to decide whether they want to be involved in the Social Security system or not. They will be free to decide whether they want a personal account or not. It will be completely voluntary. They will be able to decide how to invest their funds from a list of approved and regulated firms. They will have the freedom to leave their money to their children. They will have ownership of the personal account system. With Social Security, the worker owns nothing.

A complete shift from Social Security to a personal account system would be the largest reduction in government spending in U.S. history. It would mean the largest reduction in taxes in U.S. history. It would mean the largest reduction in government debt in U.S. history.

Social Security is an unfunded liability: $10 trillions' worth that is really government debt. It is hard to imagine a higher priority than Social Security reform. Nothing else would do so much to expand the liberty and prosperity of the American people.

Notes

[1]World Bank, "Averting the Old Age Crisis," RPO 679-63, 1994.

[2]Peter Ferrara, *Social Security: The Inherent Contradictions* (Washington, D.C.: Cato Institute), 1980.

[3]Martin Feldstein, "Privatizing Social Security: The $10 Trillion Opportunity," presented at the annual meeting of the American Economic Association, January 1996.

[4]President's Commission to Strengthen Social Security, Final report, December 21, 2001.

[5]Michael Tanner and Peter Ferrara, *A New Deal for Social Security* (Washington, D.C.: Cato Institute), 1998.

[6]Ibid.

[7]William W. Beach and Gareth G. Davis, "Social Security's Rate of Return," Heritage Foundation Center for Data Analysis Report, No. CDA 98-01, January 15, 1998.

EDWARD J. ERLER

Government vs. Bureaucracy: What Does the Constitution Say?

If we can prevent the government from wasting the labors of the people, under the pretence of taking care of them, they must become happy.

—Thomas Jefferson[1]

Today we live in what we might call the administrative state, a state where administrators regulate almost every aspect of daily life. The goal of the administrative state is to promote the welfare of the people rather than to protect its liberties—its pretense, as Jefferson noted, is "taking care" of the people. From the point of view of the administrative state, the idea that just government proceeds from the consent of the governed or that the consent of the governed is the moving principle of free government is a massive delusion. For the minions of the administrative state, the people are simply incompetent to exercise their liberties in any beneficial or just manner.

What is more, the administrative state seems to have taken on a life of its own. It appears almost unstoppable as it seeks to magnify its influence and extend the reach of its authority. Its highest imperative seems to be that the unregulated life is not worth living, to paraphrase Socrates' view of the unexamined life. The examined life and the regulated life are, of course, at opposite poles. We

119

might equate the examined life with what James Madison in the *Federalist* called "the reason . . . of the public." For it is "reason alone," Madison argued, "that ought to control and regulate the government. The passions ought to be controlled and regulated by the government."[2] Thus in Madison's view, the "reason . . . of the public" served as the foundation of the rule of law and limited government. And by limited government Madison meant a government of delegated powers. Indeed, in Madison's constitutional vision, the "reason . . . of the public" was the foundation for the moral and political order that was derived from the "consent of the governed." The administrative state, on the other hand, grounds itself in the "organic will" of the community rather than the reason of the public. And, as everyone seems to realize, government derived from "organic will" requires unlimited government since there are no reasoned limits to what can be willed.

The transformation from limited government was deliberate, a project of a group of intellectuals and politicians known as the Progressives, who did their work near the beginning of the last century. The explicit goal of Progressivism was to free the Constitution from its moorings in the founding, most particularly from what were termed the "static" doctrines of the Declaration of Independence and its reliance on the permanent truths of the "laws of nature and nature's God." Progressivism was only one form of modernity, but it shared with the other forms the depreciation of both reason and revelation as sources of moral and political authority. Progressivism was phenomenally successful in its debunking of the founding and its reformist zeal appealed wholly to the passions. It sought to liberate the passions from the constraints of the old constitutional morality that was tied to the "laws of nature and nature's God."

Woodrow Wilson, one of the leaders of Progressivism, argued that the views of the Framers had been exposed by Darwin to be hopelessly outmoded. Darwin had made it possible to replace the "static" universe that informed the politics of the Framers with one that viewed politics as a "living organism." "Liberty fixed in an unalterable law," Wilson said, "would be no liberty at all."[3] As one disciple of Wilson, the historian Richard Hofstadter, wrote in his enormously influential book *The American Political Tradition*: "no man who is as well abreast of modern science as the Fathers were of eighteenth-century science believes any longer in unchanging human nature."[4]

The constitutional device that provoked the greatest ire among the Progressives was the separation of powers. The Framers of the Constitution regarded separation of powers as an essential ingredient of limited government because it held out the prospect of securing free government as well as good government. The functional specialization of the different branches would produce good government: The multimember and diverse legislative branch would be suited for deliberation; the unitary executive suited for execution; and the insulated Supreme Court suited for judgment. Separated powers with the attendant checks and balances would operate on the principle that "ambition must be made to counteract ambition." This competition between the branches—driven by the ambitions of those who occupy the various constitutional offices—would prevent an accumulation of power in any one branch that might tend in the direction of tyranny. Thus, the separation of powers served as the principal instrument of limited government, which would be both nontyrannical and good. And, the entire constitutional scheme was meant to produce the "reason . . . of the public."

The Progressives, on the other hand, criticized separation of powers because it divided the "organic will" of the nation. Here is what Woodrow Wilson said in his 1908 treatise, "Constitutional Government":

> [G]overnment is not a machine, but a living thing. It falls, not under the theory of the universe, but under the theory of organic life. It is accountable to Darwin. . . . No living thing can have its organs offset against each other as checks, and live. On the contrary, its life is dependent upon their quick cooperation, their ready response to the commands of instinct or intelligence, their amicable community of purpose. Living political constitutions must be Darwinian in structure and in practice.[5]

Thus, from the point of view of the "organic" theory of government, separation of powers is antithetical to any "amicable community of purpose" since no living organism can be divided against itself. This progressive critique of the founding finds its most power-ful expression today in the rhetoric of the "living constitution," which must evolve and adapt to changing circumstances and especially to changing (and progressive) notions of morality. The only principle of liberty that can be recognized within the Darwinian universe is the freedom to change or progress; but it is a change or progress that has no particular end or purpose. This view makes it utterly impossible to distinguish between liberty and necessity. And it is the conflation of liberty and necessity that forms the basis of the admin-istrative state. It is necessity—or as we might say today, "needs"—not liberty and moral choice that is the motive force of the admin-istrative state.

The Progressives had simply assumed that the Framers' belief in the laws of nature had been rendered irrelevant by the progress of history. Progressive history had exposed the reliance on nature or natural right as simply the delusion of a less enlightened historical era. One could easily show that this view is theoretically inadequate. It rests on unproven (and unquestioned) assumptions that domi-nated the Progressive worldview. The Progressives failed to demon-strate why their own worldview was not simply the same kind of delusion that they claimed animated all previous historical epochs. The Progressives simply assumed that their age had produced a truth for all ages, that somehow the Progressive era was exempt from the truth that it claimed to be universal. How could the Progressives claim that all truth was relative and exempt that very statement from rela-tivity? How is it possible for one fixed and immutable truth to exist in a universe of constant change and evolution? These questions never troubled the Progressives.

The Framers, on the other hand, operated within a well-artic-ulated moral universe informed by the "laws of nature and nature's God." That is, the principles that were to animate the political and moral life of the nation were to be drawn from the principles of human nature—principles that were confirmed by biblical teach-ing. The moral universe as understood by the Framers was an artic-ulated whole, not the universe of ceaseless and aimless change that confronted the Progressives. When the Declaration of Independ-ence says that "all men are created equal, [and] that they are endowed by their Creator with certain inalienable rights," reference is made both to a Creator and a creation. Creation, of course, necessarily implies an intelligible universe, an ordered whole. While the whole may ultimately remain elusive, since God works in mysterious ways, man can discover as much of God's plan as is revealed to man's reason.

This argument was given by the Reverend Samuel West in 1776 in a sermon titled "On the Right to Rebel Against Governors"; it was an argument that was rehearsed on numerous occasions by Colonial ministers. "A revelation," Reverend West said, "pretending to be from God, that contradicts any part of the natural law, ought immediately to be rejected as an imposture, for the Deity cannot make a law contrary to the law of nature without acting contrary to himself. . . . Reason is the voice of God . . . [and] whatever right reason requires as necessary to be done is as much the will and law of God as though it were enjoined us by an immediate revelation from heaven, or commanded in the sacred Scriptures."[6]

I believe that both the argument of Reverend West and the argument of the Declaration of Independence agree with Thomas Aquinas on his account of the relation of natural law to eternal law. According to Aquinas, natural law is the rational creature's participation in eternal law, and eternal law is the law by which God governs the universe. Man participates in eternal law to the extent that he is rational; and the results of man's reasoning might properly be called natural law.

The distinction between God, man, and the lower orders of being provided the source and ground of morality in the American founding. Men do not have the perfect wisdom of God, nor are they simply creatures of instinct as are the lower animals. Thus, freedom and moral choice are the specific province of human beings.

For the Framers, constitutional morality was grounded in the "consent of the governed." The Declaration of Independence notes that the "just power" of government is derived "from the consent of the governed." It must be carefully noted that not all powers of government are derived from consent, only the "just powers." This means that at the very origin of government there is a moral requirement. Only "just powers" are authorized. And whenever government becomes unjust—that is, whenever the ends for which "just powers" have been established, the "Safety and Happiness" of the people are not protected—then the people have the natural right to withdraw their consent and "alter or abolish" the government that has assumed unjust powers.

The "consent of the governed" thus only operates legitimately when it authorizes "just powers." The establishment of government by consent is known as "social compact." Because "all men are created equal," that is, because among human beings there are no rulers by nature, only those who consent can be governed legitimately. The establishment of government thus requires unanimous consent. Once established, however, majority rule must take the place of unanimous consent, because in the operation or administration of government there will never by unanimity. One of the issues that preoccupied the Framers of the Constitution was how majority rule could be rendered just. For the Framers, the greatest danger facing popular regimes was majority faction. When a majority rules solely in the interest of the majority, the ends of just government—the protection of the safety and happiness of all who consent—are undermined. The problem is how to contrive a constitution so that the rule of the majority will be in the interest of the whole and not merely in the interest of the part. Everyone knows that the Framers relied heavily on the English philosopher John Locke for guidance in constitutional matters. In his *Second Treatise*, Locke had written about the sovereignty of the people as it manifested itself in majority rule.[7] But Locke never mentioned the dangers of majority faction—whether this was an oversight or demanded by the rhetorical stance of his work I do not venture to say. But it is clear that the Framers added a moral dimension to Locke's account by concentrating on the dangers of majority faction. Majority factions are unjust because they mistake the good of the whole of society for a part of society. The constitutional problem, as seen by the Framers, was to render the majority capable of ruling in the interest of the whole or in the common interest. As Madison phrased it, it was a problem of transforming mere numerical majorities into constitutional majorities.

"[J]ust and free government," Madison wrote, "is derived from compact." And compact, Madison said, "creates a Government" that has both "a moral power" and the "physical means of executing it." Compact, Madison explained, "contemplates a certain number of individuals as meeting and agreeing to form one political society, in order that the rights, the safety and the interest of each may be under the safeguard of the whole." After noting that compact "must result from the free consent of every individual," Madison stated that a necessary "part of the original compact" supposes that in its administration "the will of the majority was to be deemed the will of the whole." This, Madison noted, is "a law of nature, resulting from the nature of political society itself." "It is evident," Madison continued, that majority rule "operates as a plenary substitute . . . for the will of the whole society; and that the sovereignty of the society as vested in and exercisable by the majority, may do anything that could be rightfully done by the unanimous concurrence of the members; the reserved rights of individuals (of conscience, for example) in becoming parties to the original compact being beyond the legitimate reach of sovereignty, wherever vested or however viewed."[8]

Thus, the majority can only do what can be rightfully or justly done by unanimous consent. Even unanimous consent is bound by the principles of justice which put the rights of individuals "beyond the legitimate reach of sovereignty." From this point of view, the best regime would be one based on unanimity adhering to the just principles of natural law; next best would be majority rule adhering to those principles as a "plenary substitute" for unanimity.

The ground of limited government is revealed here by Madison when he remarks that "the reserved rights of individuals" are beyond the reach of sovereignty." Government must therefore be limited to securing the conditions for the exercise of rights. Madison mentions only one reserved right here, the rights of conscience or the free exercise of religion. This right is fundamental because it is the withdrawal of the rights of conscience from the sphere of government that makes majority rule possible. No member of a religious minority or any individual would accept majority determinations on issues of religion or conscience. No individual's religious opinions can be influenced by majority vote and no such vote would ever be considered legitimate by the minority. But constitutional

government depends upon the willingness of the minority to accept the legitimacy of majority rule. Thus, the separation of church
and state—the reservation of the rights of conscience—is the necessary ground for constitutional government.

What is true of the rights of conscience is also true of all the
rights that are derived from the principles of human nature. The
most comprehensive of these natural rights, according to Madison,
is the right to property. Here is what Madison had to say in his essay
"On Property" published in 1792:

> In its larger and juster meaning the right to property embraces
> every thing to which a man may attach a value and have a right;
> and which leaves to every one else the like advantage. In the
> former sense, a man's land, or merchandize, or money is called
> his property. In the latter sense, a man has a property in his
> opinions and the free communication of them. He has a
> property of a peculiar value in his religious opinions, and in
> the profession and practice dictated by them. He has a property
> very dear to him in the safety and liberty of his person. He has
> an equal property in the free use of his faculties and free choice
> of the objects on which to employ them. In a word, as a man is
> said to have a right to his property, he may be equally said to
> have a property in his rights.[9]

Madison thus viewed the rights to property as the comprehensive
right which assumed a kind of priority in the political community.

The right to property, of course, is not mentioned in the Declaration of Independence. It is a part of the "pursuit of happiness."
Here I use an Aristotelian formulation to explain the Framers' understanding of the relation between property and happiness. Property is a necessary but not a sufficient condition of happiness. Happiness requires property, but the possession of property is not the sum
total of happiness.

Life and liberty, of course, can be maintained if property is
lost. Property lost can be regained; liberty lost can be regained only
with the greatest exertions. Thus it is wise to take alarm at the slightest inroads upon the rights of property. The right to property thus

serves as a kind of "early warning system" to invasions of life and liberty. Madison's emphasis on the right of property stems from his awareness that life and liberty are mainly jeopardized through the violation of property rights—government's demands on the citizens bear most immediately and visibly on their property, whether through direct taxation, confiscation of property, or regulation of the use of property. It is therefore prudent, Madison reasoned, to make property the test and measure of liberty.

The Framers' view of the right to property, however, did not exist in a libertarian universe. Rights understood in the context of the laws of nature meant that every right carried with it a concomitant moral obligation or duty. The goal of the social compact was to protect rights and liberties by creating moral obligations based on the consent of the governed. That these obligations were freely incurred did not lessen their status as moral injunctions—indeed it served to strengthen them. Madison did not take the libertarian view of property or the libertarian view of choice. Libertarianism exists apart from moral obligations. Among a host of other considerations one would have only to refer to Madison's famous discussion of faction in the *Federalist,* no. 10: "the regulation of these various and interfering interests forms the principal task of modern legislation."[10] The principal task of modern legislation is to regulate economic activities, the various and interfering interests. But from what point of view? Surely it is to insure liberty; to prevent the dominance or monopoly of one interest which would most likely spell the end of political liberty. It is not economic liberty that is the principal task of modern legislation, but political liberty.

It is a favorite argument among some conservatives to argue that the emphasis on rights in the American founding makes it impossible to find a ground for obligation. Robert Bork, for example, asserts that the argument of the Declaration may be "pernicious" because it leads eventually "towards extremes of liberty and the pursuit of happiness that court personal license and social disorder."[11] Rights and liberties are thus understood as merely idiosyncratic preferences. But the Framers never understood the pursuit of happiness or rights generally apart from their connection to the natural law. Jefferson once spoke of the Declaration as the expression of "the American Mind." In speaking of the American Mind, Jefferson referred to a collective unity; the American mind, therefore, could not be idiosyncratic.[12] It represented a virtual consensus on the moral foundations of political liberty; it was a consensus about what constituted "public happiness." And at the core of "public happiness" was the principle that there could be no rights without concomitant obligations. It is "public happiness"—not the pursuit of idiosyncratic "values"—that is the natural law teaching of the Declaration. For the Framers, "public happiness" had an objective ground derived from the principles of human nature. Conservatives who criticize the supposed amorality of the founding have themselves rejected the idea of natural right or natural law as an effective ground of morality. Commentators like Robert Bork reject natural law principles because they do not believe that reason can play a role in the formation of morality. Natural law itself exists in the realm of values—it can have no special place in constitutional government. Bork, although claiming to adhere to the intentions of the Framers, is as far from them as the Progressives. At least the Progressives knew they were rejecting the Framers—Bork seems to be utterly unaware of it.

Let me end with a few thoughts about a Progressive-inspired reform that is currently being debated, one that constitutes a massive assault on both freedom of speech and property rights: campaign finance reform. If passed, campaign finance reform will go far in the direction of consolidating the power of the administrative state. Free elections, of course, are the hallmark of republican government; but all too often the electorate has resisted attempts to extend the power and reach of the administrative state. Indeed, particularly in recent years the electorate seems to prefer smaller and more limited government. This recalcitrance on the part of the electorate, I believe, has been a great spur to reform efforts.

Richard Gephardt, the minority leader in the House of Representatives, recently made this startling announcement: "What we have here is two important values in conflict: freedom of speech and our desire for healthy campaigns in a healthy democracy. You can't have both."[13] Gephardt proceeded to cosponsor an amendment to the Constitution that would have repealed important provisions of the First Amendment's guarantee of freedom of speech. What were the two values in conflict? Freedom of speech on the one hand and "healthy campaigns" on the other. For Gephardt and the supporters of reform, a "healthy" election is one where campaign expenditures are limited in the name of "fairness." As a matter of fairness, we are told, those who are wealthy should not have greater access to political speech. As one prominent academic advocate of reform says, "laws that restrict expenditures on campaigns have been justified as an effort to promote political deliberation and political equality by reducing the distorting effects of disparities in wealth."[14] Supporters of reform dismiss First Amendment concerns with unabashed casualness. As I mentioned earlier, the highest imperative of the administrative state is not liberty, but rather a complete regime of regulation. Campaign finance reform shows the administrative state at its worst, working by indirection and deception.

It is said that the goal of campaign finance regulation is twofold: to reduce corruption or the appearance of corruption and to equalize the relative abilities of individuals to influence the outcome of elections. Reformers believe that any system of private campaign financing will be corrupt because it translates inequality of wealth into inequality of political power and influence. Thus, public financing of elections or severe limits on campaign spending are said to be imperative to deliberative democracy. Reform will increase access to electoral politics, we are told, and will give a more egalitarian cast to the electoral process. And to the extent that it is more egalitarian and less corrupt, it will be more just. No system of private campaign financing can be egalitarian, of course, because in a free society there will inevitably be wealth disparities. Because "healthy" campaigns will not reflect the influence of wealth, such campaigns will themselves eventually become a factor in the redistribution of wealth. Thus, in the eyes of the minions of the administrative state, the exercise of the right to property is somehow incompatible with the right to liberty. In their eyes, Madison was wrong when he argued that there was no incompatibility of the two rights because every individual, in addition to a natural right to property, had a property in his rights, especially the free communication of ideas.

Government control over campaign finance will inevitably mean government control over politics. Government regulation of campaign finance is inseparable from government control of the electoral process itself. In this sense, government will not be just a neutral regulator but a faction with an interest to promote—the extension and perpetuation of the administrative state.

In 1976, the Supreme Court heard a challenge to the Federal Election Campaign Act of 1971. In *Buckley* v. *Valeo*, the Court invalidated portions of the act that put spending limits on the direct expression of political opinion, but upheld contribution limits unrelated to direct expression. The Court reasoned that "every means of communicating ideas in today's mass society requires the expenditure of money." But the Court noted that it violated the core principles of the First Amendment to "restrict the speech of some elements . . . in order to enhance the relative voice of others." Indeed, the Court said, "the First Amendment denied government the power to determine that spending to promote one's political views is wasteful, excessive or unwise. In the free society ordained by our Constitution, it is not the government but the people—individually as citizens and candidates and collectively as associations and political committees—who must retain control over the quantity and range of debate on public issues in a political campaign."[15] While the Court was undoubtedly right in this statement of general principle, it is difficult to justify the distinction it made between campaign contributions and campaign expenditures. The Court said that there could be no restrictions on the amount of money a candidate spent on his own behalf or on the amount an independent organization could spend on behalf of a candidate. The Court ruled that in these instances, First Amendment liberties were implicated because the money was spent directly on expressive activities. Contributions, on the other hand, were used to promote the speech of someone else and could therefore be limited and regulated. The precise distinction made here by the Court utterly escapes me. I believe that contributions to finance the speech of those with whom you agree or wish to promote are no less speech activities than if you use the money for your own speech. If I give money to someone—say a young and relatively unknown successor to Abraham Lincoln—who can articulate my political ideas better than I can, these are no less my political ideas than if I gave voice to them myself. In my opinion, the distinction between spending and contributions is not mandated by any known principle of First Amendment jurisprudence and is certainly alien to the Framers' understanding of both property and political liberty.

Everyone seems to realize that restrictions on campaign spending favor incumbents. Far from equalizing access to the electoral process, spending limits work in the favor of those who already hold office; it makes challenges difficult. The incumbent has name recognition and can use all the advantages of office-holding to keep himself in power. Complex election regulations and reporting requirements make it difficult for challengers; the start-up costs are enormous and much of the limited spending must be used for high administrative costs. Incumbents are not unaware of the advantages of campaign finance regulations—why else propose that most political advertising be banned 60 days before the election, that is, at the time when it matters most? Only a few politicians dare to point out the First Amendment implications of reform—Gephardt was unusually honest (or unusually confident) when he called for the repeal of the First Amendment's protection of political speech. After all, the surface attractions of reform seem to be popular; what reform promises, however, it simply cannot deliver. Reform works to the advantage of incumbency and a career in politics may be a greater spur to corruption than campaign contributions.

Campaign finance reform co-opts politicians into the administrative state. In return for powerful incumbency protection, politicians are eager to transfer a significant portion of First Amendment liberties to the administrative state. As Madison might have argued, this is a cure that is worse than the disease.

Notes

[1] Letter to Thomas Cooper, November 29, 1802, in Merrill D. Peterson, ed., *Jefferson: Writings* (New York: Library of America, 1984), p. 1110.
[2] James Madison, *Federalist*, No. 49, Clinton Rossiter, ed.; Introduction and notes by Charles Kesler (New York: Mentor Books, 1999).

[3]Woodrow Wilson, "Constitutional Government," in Arthur S. Link, ed., *The Papers of Woodrow Wilson*, vol. 18 (Princeton, NJ: Princeton University Press, 1968), p. 71

[4]Richard Hofstadter, *The American Political Tradition* (New York: Random House, 1973), pp. 16–17.

[5]"Constitutional Government," in *The Papers of Woodrow Wilson*, vol. 18, p. 106.

[6]Reverend Samuel West, "On the Right to Rebel against Governors," in Charles S. Hyneman and Donald S. Lutz, eds., *American Political Writings during the Founding Era, 1760–1860*, vol. 1 (Indianapolis, IN: Liberty Press, 1983), p. 416.

[7]John Locke, *Second Treatise*, Peter Laslett, ed. (New York: Cambridge University Press, 1988), par. 96.

[8]James Madison, "Sovereignty," in Gaillard Hunt, ed., *The Writings of James Madison*, vol. 9 (New York: G. P. Putnam's Sons, 1910), pp. 569–71.

[9]James Madison, "On Property," in Robert Rutland et al., eds., *The Papers of James Madison*, vol. 14 (Charlottesville, VA: University Press of Virginia, 1983), p. 266.

[10]James Madison, *Federalist*, No. 10, p. 47.

[11]Robert H. Bork, *Slouching Towards Gomorrah* (New York: Regan Books, 1996), p. 57.

[12]Thomas Jefferson, Letter to Henry Lee, May 8, 1825, in *Jefferson: Writings*, p. 1501.

[13]Richard Gephardt, quoted in Bradley A. Smith, *Unfree Speech: The Folly of Campaign Finance Reform* (Princeton, NJ: Princeton University Press, 2001), p. 10.

[14]Cass R. Sunstein, *The Partial Constitution* (Cambridge, MA: Harvard University Press, 1993), p. 223.

[15]*Buckley v. Valeo*, 414 U.S. 1, at 19, 48–9, 57 (1976).

LUDWIG VON MISES

The Bureaucratic vs. the Market Principle in Business Management

The opposition between the commercial and the bureaucratic mentality is the counterpart in the intellectual realm of the opposition between capitalism—private ownership of the means of production—and socialism—communal ownership of the means of production. Whoever has factors of production at his disposal, whether his own or those lent to him by their owners in return for some compensation, must always be careful to employ them in such a way as to satisfy those needs of society that, under the given circumstances, are the most urgent. If he does not do this, he will operate at a loss and will find himself at first under the necessity of curtailing his activity as owner and entrepreneur and ultimately ousted from that position altogether. He ceases to be the one or the other and has to fall back into the ranks of those who have only their labor to sell and who do not have the responsibility of guiding production into those channels that, from the point of view of the consumers, are the right ones. In the calculation of profits and losses, which constitutes the whole sum and substance of the businessman's bookkeeping and accounting, entrepreneurs and capitalists possess a method that enables them to check, with the greatest attainable exactitude, every step in their procedure down to the smallest detail and, where possible, to see what effect each individual trans-

From Ludwig von Mises, *Liberalism: The Classical Tradition* (Irvington-on-Hudson, NY: The Foundation for Economic Education, Inc., 1966), pp. 96–104. Reprinted with permission.

action in the conduct of their operations will have on the total outcome of the enterprise. Monetary calculation and cost accounting
constitute the most important intellectual tool of the capitalist entrepreneur, and it was no one less than Goethe who pronounced
the system of double-entry bookkeeping "one of the finest inventions of the human mind." Goethe could say this because he was
free from the resentment that the petty literati always foster against
the businessman. It is they that form the chorus whose constant
refrain is that monetary calculation and concern with profit and
loss are the most shameful of sins.

Monetary calculation, bookkeeping and statistics on sales and
operations make it possible for even the biggest and most complex
business concerns to make an exact check on the results achieved
in every single department and thereby to form a judgment on the
extent to which the head of each department has contributed to
the total success of the enterprise. Thus, a reliable guide is provided for determining the treatment to be accorded to the managers
of the various departments. One can know what they are worth and
how much they are to be paid. Advancement to higher and more
responsible positions is by way of unquestionably demonstrated success in a more circumscribed sphere of action. And just as one is
able to check on the activity of the manager of each department by
means of cost accounting, so one can also scrutinize the activity of
the enterprise in every single field of its over-all operation, as well
as the effects of certain organizational and similar measures.

There are, to be sure, limits to this exact control. One cannot
determine the success or failure of the activity of each individual
within a department as one can that of its manager. There are, be-
sides, departments whose contribution to the total output cannot
be comprehended by means of calculation: what a research department, a legal bureau, a secretariat, a statistical service, etc., accom-
plishes cannot be ascertained in the same way as, for instance, the
performance of a particular sales or production department. The
former may be quite safely left to the approximate estimation of
the person in charge of the department, and the latter to that of
the general manager of the concern; for conditions can be seen
with relative clarity and those who are called upon to make these

judgments (both the general management and that of the various departments) have a personal interest in their correctness, as their own incomes are affected by the productivity of the operations of which they are in charge.

The opposite of this type of enterprise, whose every transaction is controlled by the calculation of profit and loss, is represented by the apparatus of public administration. Whether a judge (and what is true of a judge is true in the same way of every high administrative official) has discharged his duties better or worse cannot be demonstrated by any computation. There is no possible way of establishing by an objective criterion whether a district or a province is being administered well or badly, cheaply or expensively. The judgment of the activity of public officials is thus a matter of subjective, and therefore quite arbitrary, opinion. Even the question whether a particular bureau is necessary, whether it has too many or too few employees, and whether its organization is or is not suited to its purpose can be decided only on the basis of considerations that involve some element of subjectivity. There is but one field of public administration in which the criterion of successor failure is unquestionable: the waging of war. But even here the only thing certain is whether the operation has been crowned with success. The question how far the distribution of power determined the issue even before the beginning of hostilities and how much of the outcome is to be attributed to the competence or incompetence of the leaders in their conduct of the operations and to the appropriateness of the measures they took cannot be strictly and precisely answered. There have been generals celebrated for their victories who, in fact, did everything to facilitate the triumph of the enemy and who owe their success solely to circumstances so favorable as to outweigh their mistakes. And vanquished leaders have sometimes been condemned whose genius had done everything possible to prevent the inevitable defeat.

The manager of a private enterprise gives the employees to whom he assigns independent duties only one directive: to make as much profit as possible. Everything that he has to say to them is comprehended in this one order, and an examination of the accounts makes it possible to determine easily and accurately to what extent they have followed it. The manager of a bureaucratic department finds himself in a quite different situation. He can tell his subordinates what they have to accomplish, but he is not in a position to ascertain whether the means employed for the attainment of this result are the most appropriate and economical under the circumstances. If he is not omnipresent in all the offices and bureaus subordinate to him, he cannot judge whether the attainment of the same result would not have been possible with a lesser expenditure of labor and materials. The fact that the result itself is also not amenable to numerical measurement, but only to approximate assessment, need not be discussed here. For we are not considering administrative technique from the point of view of its external effects, but merely from the standpoint of its reaction upon the internal operation of the bureaucratic apparatus; we are concerned with the result attained, therefore, only in its relation to the expenses incurred.

Because it is out of the question to undertake to determine this relationship by means of computations after the manner of commercial bookkeeping, the manager of a bureaucratic organization must provide his subordinates with instructions with which compliance is made obligatory. In these instructions provision is made, in a general way, for the ordinary and regular course of business. In all extraordinary cases, however, before any money is spent, permission must first be obtained from higher authority—a tedious and rather ineffectual procedure in favor of which all that can be said is that it is the only method possible. For if every subaltern bureau, every department head, every branch office, were given the right to make the expenditures that they deemed requisite, the costs of administration would soon soar without limit. One should not delude oneself about the fact that this system is seriously defective and very unsatisfactory. Many expenses are incurred that are superfluous, and many that would be necessary are not made because a bureaucratic apparatus cannot, by its very nature, adjust itself to circumstances as a commercial organization can.

The effect of bureaucratization is most apparent in its representative—the bureaucrat. In a private enterprise, the hiring of labor is not the conferring of a favor, but a business transaction from which both parties, employer and employee, benefit. The employer must endeavor to pay wages corresponding in value to the labor performed. If he does not do this, he runs the risk of seeing the worker leave his employment for that of a better-paying competitor. The employee, in order not to lose his job, must in his turn endeavor to fulfill the duties of his position well enough to be worth his wages. Since employment is not a favor, but a business transaction, the employee does not need to fear that he may be discharged if he falls into personal disfavor. For the entrepreneur who discharges, for reasons of personal bias, a useful employee who is worth his pay harms only himself and not the worker, who can find a similar position elsewhere. There is not the slightest difficulty in entrusting to the manager of each department the authority to hire and fire employees; for under the pressure of the control exercised over his activities by bookkeeping and cost accounting he must see to it that his department shows as great a profit as possible, and hence he is obliged, in his own interest, to be careful to retain the best employees there. If out of spite he discharges someone whom he ought not to have discharged, if his actions are motivated by personal, and not objective, considerations, then it is he himself who must suffer the consequences. Any impairment of the success of the department headed by him must ultimately redound to his loss. Thus, the incorporation of the nonmaterial factor, labor, into the process of production takes place without any friction.

In a bureaucratic organization things are quite different. Since the productive contribution of the individual department and hence also of the individual employee, even when he occupies an executive position, cannot in this case be ascertained, the door is wide open to favoritism and personal bias both in appointment and remuneration. The fact that the intercession of influential persons plays a certain role in filling official positions in the civil service is not due to a peculiar baseness of character on the part of those responsible for filling these posts, but to the fact that from the very outset there is no objective criterion for determining an individual's qualification for appointment. Of course, it is the most competent who ought to be employed, but the question is: Who is the most competent? If this question could be as easily answered as the question what an ironworker or a compositor is worth, there would be no problem. But since this is not the case, an element of arbitrariness is necessarily involved in comparing the qualifications of different individuals.

In order to keep this within the narrowest possible limits, one seeks to set up formal conditions for appointment and promotion. Attainment to a particular position is made dependent on the fulfillment of certain educational requirements, on the passing of examinations, and on continued employment for a certain period of time in other positions; promotion is made dependent on years of previous service. Naturally, all these expedients are in no sense a substitute for the possibility of finding the best available man for every post by means of the calculation of profit and loss. It would be supererogatory to point out in particular that the attendance at school, examinations, and seniority do not offer the slightest guarantee that the selection will be correct. On the contrary: this system from the very outset prevents the energetic and the competent from occupying positions in line with their powers and capabilities. Never yet has anyone of real worth risen to the top by way of a prescribed program of study and promotion in due course along the established lines. Even in Germany, which has a pious faith in her bureaucrats, the expression, "a perfection functionary," is used to connote a spineless and ineffectual person, however well intentioned.

Thus, the characteristic mark of bureaucratic management is that it lacks the guidance provided by consideration of profit and loss in judging the success of its operations in relation to the expenses incurred and is consequently obliged, in the effort to compensate for this deficiency, to resort to the entirely inadequate expedient of making its conduct of affairs and the hiring of its personnel subject to a set of formal prescriptions. All the evils that are commonly imputed to bureaucratic management—its inflexibility, its lack of resourcefulness, and its helplessness in the face of problems that are easily solved in a profit-seeking enterprise—are the result of this one fundamental deficiency. As long as the activity of the state is restricted to the narrow field that liberalism assigns to it, the disadvantages of bureaucracy cannot, at any rate, make themselves too apparent. They become a grave problem for the whole economy only when the state—and naturally the same is true of municipalities and other forms of local government—proceeds to socialize the means of production and to take an active part in it or even in trade.

A public enterprise conducted with an eye to maximizing profits can, to be sure, make use of monetary calculation as long as most business is privately owned and hence a market still exists and market prices are formed. The only hindrance to its operation and development is the fact that its managers, as functionaries of the state, do not have the personal interest in the success or failure of the business that is characteristic of the management of private enterprises. The director cannot, therefore, be given freedom to act independently in making crucial decisions. Since he would not suffer the losses that could result, under certain circumstances, from his business policy, his conduct of affairs could all too easily be disposed to run risks that would not be taken by a director who, because he must share in the loss, is genuinely responsible. His authority must, therefore, be in some way limited. Whether it is bound by a set of rigid regulations or the decisions of a control council or the consent of a superior authority, bureaucratic management in any case continues to suffer from the unwieldiness and the lack of ability to adjust itself to changing conditions that have everywhere led public enterprises from one failure to another.

But, in fact, it is only seldom that a public enterprise aims at nothing but profit and sets aside all other considerations. As a rule, it is demanded of a public enterprise that it keep in mind certain "national" and other considerations. It is expected, for instance, in its procurement and sales policy, to favor domestic as against foreign production. It is demanded of state railways that they set a schedule of rates that will serve a specific commercial policy on the part of the government, that they construct and maintain lines that cannot be profitably operated simply in order to promote the economic development of a certain area, and that they operate certain others for strategic or similar reasons. When such factors play a role in the conduct of a business, all control by the methods of cost accounting and the calculation of profit and loss is out of the question. The director of the state railways who presents an unfavorable balance sheet at the end of the year is in a position to say: "The railway lines under my supervision have, to be sure, operated at a loss if considered from the strictly commercial point of view of profit-seeking private enterprise; but if one takes into consideration such factors as our national economic and military policy, one must not forget that they have accomplished a great deal that does not enter into the calculation of profit and loss." Under such circumstances the calculation of profit and loss has clearly lost all value for judging the success of an enterprise, so that—even apart from other factors having the same tendency—it must necessarily be managed quite as bureaucratically as, for example, the administration of a prison or a tax bureau.

No private enterprise, whatever its size, can ever become bureaucratic as long as it is entirely and solely operated on a profit basis. Firm adherence to the entrepreneurial principle of aiming at the highest profit makes it possible for even the largest concern to ascertain with complete precision the part played by every transaction and by the activity of every department in contribution to the total result. As long as enterprises look only to profit, they are proof against all the evils of bureaucratism. The bureaucratization of privately owned enterprises that we see going on about us everywhere today is purely the result of interventionism, which forces them to take into account factors that, if they were free to determine their policies for themselves, would be far from playing any role whatsoever in the conduct of their business. When a concern must pay heed to political prejudices and sensibilities of all kinds in order to avoid being continually harassed by various organs of the state, it soon finds that it is no longer in a position to base its calculations on the solid ground of profit and loss. For instance, some of the public utility enterprises in the United States, in order to avoid conflicts with public opinion and with the legislative, judicial, and administrative organs of the government which it influences, make it a policy not to hire Catholics, Jews, atheists, Darwinists, Negroes, Irishmen, Germans, Italians, and all newly arrived immigrants. In the interventionist state, every business is under the necessity of accommodating itself to the wishes of the authorities in order to avoid burdensome penalties. The result is that these and other considerations foreign to the profit-seeking principles of entrepreneurial management come to play an every increasing role in the conduct of business, while the part played by precise calculation and cost accounting concomitantly dwindles in significance, and private enterprise begins increasingly to adopt the mode of management of public enterprises, with their elaborate apparatus of formally prescribed rules and regulations. In a word, it becomes bureaucratized.

Thus, the progressing bureaucratization of big business is by no means the result of an inexorable tendency inherent in the development of the capitalist economy. It is nothing but the necessary consequence of adopting a policy of interventionism. In the absence of government interference with their operations, even the largest firms could be run in exactly as businesslike a way as the small ones.